The Politics of Nationalism and Ethnicity

The Politics of Nationalism and Ethnicity

James G. Kellas

MACMILLAN

First published 1991

Published by
MACMILLAN EDUCATION LTD
Houndmills, Basingstoke, Hampshire RG21 2XS
and London
Companies and representatives
throughout the world

Printed in Hong Kong

British Library Cataloguing in Publication Data
Kellas, James G.
The Politics of Nationalism and Ethnicity
1. Nationalism
I. Title
320.54
ISBN   0–333–45256–9
ISBN   0–333–45257–7   pbk

Contents

List of Tables

Acknowledgements

I first studied nationalism as an undergraduate student of Joseph Frankel at the University of Aberdeen in 1957–58, and later specialised in the study of Scottish politics as a university lecturer. Once more, the subject of nationalism came to the fore, in the form of Scottish nationalism. As a Visiting Professor of Political Science at the University of Pittsburgh in 1985–86, I taught a course on nationalism generally, and had regular discussions on the subject with Richard Cottam (an expert on Middle East nationalism), Dennison Rusinow (an historian with a particular interest in Balkan nationalism), and Christina Paulston (a linguist specialising in language survival). These sessions broadened my perspective considerably.

At the University of Glasgow, I have kept up a continuous discourse on nationalism with colleagues, many of whom are experts on political theory and the study of particular areas of the world. Most of these will perhaps be surprised at the content of this book, and perhaps alarmed. I hope they do not mind my thanking them here, but they are of course not a party to what I have written.

Special thanks are due to Mrs Avril Johnstone, who coped with the frequent revisions during the production of the typescript.

Introduction

Nationalism and ethnicity are central to the subject of politics, whether in the world of action or in the realm of study. Countless wars, revolts and conflicts have been the result of the passions which nation and 'kith and kin' have aroused in human beings. It has been estimated that more than ten million lives have been lost since 1945 alone as a result of ethnic violence (Horowitz, 1985, p. xi, quoting Isaacs, 1975, p. 3). That total has probably risen by another million since 1975, and may in fact be on the increase. Two thousand died in 1989 alone in ethnic violence in the Punjab, and as many in Sri Lanka. Deaths and injuries because of ethnic violence have also been common in Azerbaijan, Kashmir, Burma in Asia, and the Basque country and Northern Ireland in Europe, to name only a few examples. Nationalist passions are probably the strongest in the whole political spectrum, and are generally stronger today than those aroused by religion, class, individual or group interest.

These passions are not all negative, however. Nationalism has been considered essential to the establishment of a modern industrial society (Gellner, 1983). It gives legitimacy to the state, and inspires its citizens to feel an emotional attachment towards it. It can be a source of creativity in the arts, and enterprise in the economy. Its power to mobilise political activity is unsurpassed, especially in the vital activity of 'nation-building'.

The student of politics is faced with many problems when tackling this subject. Not only are the manifestations of nationalism and ethnicity widespread and complex, but there is also a very large and contradictory literature in this field, with works by sociologists, philosophers and historians as well as by political scientists. This is understandable, given the universal scope and importance of the subject. But the spread across disciplines has tended to produce not so much a synthesis as several partial views. In the case of political science, it is not clear that there is a distinctive view at all. Certainly, there is no integrated theory of the politics of nationalism which, while taking account of the many theories relating to the subject, focuses especially on the political dimension and

1

produces an integrated theoretical analysis. This is especially needed, as it is politics which gives the most powerful expression to nations and ethnic groups.

While this book attempts to develop such a theory, it also aims to provide an introduction to, and explain, all the major approaches to the subject. Some of these approaches are mutually exclusive, but others can complement each other. For example, while it is difficult to reconcile the view that human nature leads to nationalism with the view that nationalism arose in a specific period in history, it is possible to show that nationalist behaviour has both cultural and economic determinants. This reconciles some linguistic studies of nationalism with certain Marxist writers. For political scientists, the focus is on the state and political power. Nationalism and ethnic politics are related to the state and the struggle for control of political resources. Thus the agenda stretches to constitutions, parties, groups, leaders and voters. These interact with the cultural and economic forces and may explain when nationalism is successful and when it is not.

Definitions

A serious problem for students of the subject is the ambiguity in the meaning of the words used. At this stage, the reader will find it useful to consider the following basic terms, which will recur throughout this book. As there is no agreed meaning for them, rather an emerging consensus in the literature, it cannot be claimed that a 'correct' meaning is given here. But a working definition of each is essential for further study (a major glossary of concepts and terms in the study of ethnicity has been prepared by Professor F. W. Riggs of the University of Hawaii, under the auspices of the International Social Science Council's Committee on Conceptual and Terminological Analysis [INTERCOCTA]) (Riggs, 1985).

Nation. A nation is a group of people who feel themselves to be a community bound together by ties of history, culture, and common ancestry. Nations have 'objective' characteristics which may include a territory, a language, a religion, or common descent (though not all of these are always present), and 'subjective' characteristics, essentially a people's awareness of its nationality and affection for it. In the last resort it is 'the supreme loyalty' for people who are prepared to die for their nation.

The term nation is also commonly applied to states, as in the United Nations, consisting of the 'nations' of the world. While many states share the features of nations, and can be called 'nation-states', there are also nations within states, and such states are correctly called 'multinational states'. For centuries there were multinational empires such as the Austrian, Ottoman and Russian Empires, and today there are states consisting of more than one nation such as the United Kingdom, Switzerland, Belgium and Canada. The USSR is composed of over one hundred 'nationalities', and this term is officially preferred there to 'nations', for political reasons. 'Nations' in communist ideology are linked to nationalism, with the possible break-up of the state, while 'nationalities' are expected to have predominantly cultural aspirations.

In this work, 'nation' is used independently of 'state' and 'ethnic group', but these terms overlap in some cases. For example, Denmark, Iceland and Japan are states in which nearly all the citizens belong to one nation, meaning a social community. That nation can also be analysed in terms of ethnicity, but as will shortly be explained, 'ethnic group' has special connotations in contemporary politics. In some works, the terms 'ethnonation' and 'ethnonationalism' are used to distinguish an ethnic nation and ethnic nationalism from 'nation' meaning state, and 'nationalism' meaning patriotism. Here, **'ethnic nation'** is used where a nation consists of one ethnic group, **'social nation'** where several ethnic groups form one nation, and **'official nation'** for the nationalism of the state.

Nationalism. Nationalism is both an ideology and a form of behaviour. The ideology of nationalism builds on people's awareness of a nation ('national self-consciousness') to give a set of attitudes and a programme of action. These may be cultural, economic, or political. Since 'nation' can be defined in 'ethnic', 'social' or 'official' senses, so nationalism can take these forms also.

In all cases, nationalism seeks to defend and promote the interests of the nation. The political aspect of nationalism is seen most clearly in the demand for 'national self-determination', or 'home rule'. For states, 'official nationalism' means patriotism and the defence of 'national sovereignty' in international relations. All types of nationalism seek a political expression for the nation, most strongly in independent statehood. Nationalists may settle for less, however. They may be content (at least, for a time) for the nation to be a unit in a federal state (e.g., Armenia in the USSR and Quebec in Canada) or to have devolution in a unitary state (e.g., Wales in the UK and Catalonia in Spain). It must be said, however, that not all federalists or devolutionists would recognise themselves as nationalists, for many would see nationalism as undesirable since it could lead to the disintegration of the state. Lastly, nationalists, especially ethnic nationalists, may engage only in 'pressure group' politics, with no territorial aim regarding 'home rule'. Their aim is rather the protection and advancement of the ethnic group within the state.

As a form of political behaviour, nationalism is closely linked to ethnocentrism (see below) and patriotism. Nationalist behaviour is based on the feeling of belonging to a community which is the nation. Those who do not belong to the nation are seen as different, foreigners or aliens, with loyalties to their own nations. Nationalist behaviour in its strongest form is seen in the 'supreme sacrifice' of death for one's nation. In milder forms, it shows itself in prejudice relating to foreigners, stereotyping of other nations, and solidarity with co-nationals. 'Official nationalism' or patriotism is sometimes given a more noble status than other forms of nationalism, and may conflict with these. Patriotism focuses loyalty on the state, while 'social' and 'ethnic' nationalism may seek the disintegration of the state.

Ethnic group. 'Ethnic group' and 'ethnocentrism' are comparable with 'nation' and 'nationalism'. The difference between them is that 'ethnic group' is more narrowly defined than 'nation', and 'ethnocentrism' is more rooted in social psychology than is 'nationalism', which has explicitly ideological and political dimensions. Ethnic groups are generally differentiated from nations on several dimensions: they are usually smaller; they are more clearly based on a common ancestry; and they are more pervasive in human history, while nations are perhaps specific to time and place. Ethnic groups are essentially **exclusive** or **ascriptive**, meaning that membership in such groups is confined to those who share certain inborn attributes. Nations on the other hand are more *inclusive* and are culturally or politically defined. However, it is often possible to trace the origins of nations and nationalism to ethnic groups and their ethnocentric behaviour (Kohn, 1944; Smith, 1986).

In contemporary political usage, the term 'ethnic group' is frequently used to describe a quasi-national kind of 'minority group' within the state, which has somehow not achieved the status of a 'nation'. Thus, 'ethnic politics' in Britain means the politics of recent non-white immigrants, while 'nationalism' is applied to the English, Scots, Welsh and Irish. The English are often considered in England to be neither 'ethnic' nor 'nationalist', rather 'patriotic'. Other people may see the English as ethnic and nationalist, and the English themselves show themselves to be such in politics, particularly with regard to the other nations of the United Kingdom, or to the black population in England.

'Race Relations' is yet another dimension involved here. 'Race' is distinguished from 'nation' and 'ethnic group' mainly because 'races' are discussed in predominantly biological terms, with particular emphasis on 'phenotypical' distinctions such as skin colour, stature, etc, and presumed genetic distinctions. **'Racism'** matches 'nationalism' as an ideology and type of behaviour, and is related to 'race' rather than to 'nation'. It is even more negatively assessed generally than nationalism, and has led to political action to counteract it (e.g., race relations legislation, civil rights movements, anti-apartheid campaigns, etc).

Ethnocentrism. 'Ethnocentrism' is basically a psychological term, although it is also used generally in the study of society and politics. It can be related to 'nationalism' and 'racism', but its focus is strictly on the individual's relationship with an ethnic group rather than with a 'nation' or a 'race'. Ethnocentrism gives a general and perhaps even universal basis for a type of behaviour which also underlies nationalism and racism. It is essentially concerned with an individual's psychological biases towards his/her ethnic group, and against other ethnic groups. Favourable attitudes are held about the 'ingroup' (here the ethnic group, nation, or race), and unfavourable ones about the 'outgroup' (other ethnic groups, nations or races). The intensity of ethnocentric attitudes and behaviour varies from the mild and peaceful to the belligerent and megalomaniac (van der Dennen in Reynolds, 1987, p. 1). The causes of ethnocentrism in general and the explanations for its different forms are complex and have been the subject of various sociobiological, psychological and sociological studies (see for example, LeVine and Campbell, 1972; Adorno, 1950; Forbes, 1985; Reynolds *et al.*, 1987).

Ethnicity. Ethnicity is the state of being ethnic, or belonging to an ethnic group. It is a more neutral term than ethnocentrism which, as we have seen, denotes prejudicial attitudes favouring one ethnic group and rejecting others. While some nations may be called 'ethnic nations', there are ethnic groups who do not claim to be nations. The difference may be found in the character of ethnic politics compared with nationalist politics. Nationalism focuses on 'national self-determination', or home rule in a national territory. Ethnic politics in contrast are largely concerned with the protection of rights for members of the group within the existing state, with no claim for a territorial 'homeland'. However, these distinctions are not made by all scholars. The field of 'ethnic studies' include nations and nationalism, and many nations have 'ethnic origins' (Smith, 1986).

Argument

The central aim of this book is to provide an '**integrated theory of the politics of nationalism and ethnicity**'. The theory is constructed from 'building-blocks' which lead in sequence from one to the other. Within each building-block are posited 'necessary' and 'sufficient' conditions. A full treatment of this theory is given in the concluding chapter, and a synopsis of it in tabular form at the end.

Essentially, the theory starts with the hypothesis of a link between certain traits in human nature and ethnicity and ethnocentrism. Nationalism and ethnic politics display characteristics of emotion and intensity which appear to derive from instinctive behaviour, and from a human predisposition to show loyalty to 'ingroups' and hostility to 'outgroups' (ethnocentrism).

Particular ethnic groups and nations become such groups through informal processes of interaction, and from the more sophisticated influence of nationalist ideology and political structures, especially states. 'Nationalism' is an ideology which claims supreme loyalty from individuals for the nation and asserts the right of 'national self-determination' or self-government for the nation. There are other nationalist ideologies which make claims for the nation, such as its inherent superiority to other nations. Their appeal is based on an analogy between nations and 'kin', and they tap instinctive feelings of ethnocentrism.

The context in which nationalism flourishes is determined by a complex interaction of political, economic and cultural developments in history. While the ideology of nationalism has spread throughout the world, the differing contexts of time and place have given nationalism and ethnicity differing political forms. A particularly strong explanation of nationalist behaviour is that which relates it to perceptions of 'uneven economic development' affecting different nations and ethnic groups, coupled with a 'Cultural Division of Labour'. But the political aspirations for democracy, and cultural changes (e.g., widespread education and a desire for cultural status) are as important.

The democratic alternative to nationalist ideology is cultural pluralism and consociationalism, based on a multinational or multiethnic 'consensus' state. For such a state to succeed, certain strategies must be adopted. In international relations, supranationalism and 'integration' face similar obstacles, and consociationalism there is more difficult to achieve. Yet strategies for international integration can also be devised.

Structure of the book

The chapters of the book are based on the 'building-blocks' of the theory. Chapter 1 discusses **human nature** (biology and psychology) and its connection with ethnicity and ethnocentrism. Chapter 2 describes the emergence of the **idea of the nation and the ideology of nationalism**. Chapters 3, 4, and 5 put these in a **historical context**, with generalisation about **types** of nationalisms and nationalist movements. Chapters 6, 7, and 8 deal with contemporary **case studies** of nationalism and ethnic politics, distinguishing between different parts of the world. Chapter 9 looks at **cultural pluralism**, **consociational democracy** and other methods of **political accommodation** in a multinational and multiethnic state. Chapter 10 discusses nationalism in **international relations**. Chapter 11 describes the **integrated theory** of the politics of nationalism and ethnicity.

1

Ethnicity and Human Nature

The most difficult and controversial part of the study of nationalism is trying to find a general explanation for its existence. Scholars are divided into those who go back to something called 'human nature', where instinctive behaviour is to be found, and those who look only for historical, cultural and economic explanations ('contexts'). The former have the problem that what is universally true is not much use in explaining particular differences in the world. The latter have great difficulty in explaining why the passions aroused by nationalism are so strong and universal, so that they seem to transcend mere 'circumstances' to tap deep-seated emotions.

In this chapter we look at writings on nationalism and ethnicity which focus on human nature, but we shall also take account of the arguments against such an approach. On balance, this book accepts that human nature (insofar as that can be defined) plays some part in explaining why ethnicity and nationalism have been so pervasive and powerful in human history. But the evidence is ambiguous, and some readers may prefer to reject this part of the theory (see Synopsis, at end). In any case, in the theory human nature is only a 'necessary condition' for the many manifestations of nationalism and ethnic politics in history. Why particular nations and nationalisms develop is a matter for historical explanation. Thus, for there to be 'sufficient conditions' in any particular case relating to nationalism and ethnicity, explanations which go beyond human nature must be invoked.

Yet the basic question remains: why should people distrust and dislike foreigners, and prefer 'their own kind'? Why does nationalism lead to wars and legitimise 'the supreme sacrifice', to die for one's country? Is Robert Burns to be believed when he wrote:

8

'It's coming yet, for a' that,
That man to man, the warld o'er,
Shall brothers be for a' that.'?

This is rhetoric which invokes the extension of family ties to humanity as a whole. 'The Brotherhood of Man' has inspired 'universalists' in politics, and has led to institutions such as the United Nations, with its 'Universal Declaration of Human Rights' (1948). But in the rhetoric of nationalism 'brotherhood' means something different from sympathy and common interest with one's fellow human beings; it implies a closer blood relationship ('brothers-in-law' are of course not usually close blood relations, but 'brothers' of a kind, nevertheless).

Blood relationships are fundamental to life and to reproduction. Politics is concerned intimately with the impact which such relationships have on human beings. We all understand what 'father' and 'mother' means, as well as 'brother', 'sister' and 'cousin'. Even more distant relations can arouse sympathy and lead to 'nepotism' (favouring one's relations). The whole 'family' is a ready-made structure from our basic experience, which can be translated into politics (the 'British family of nations'). The 'Fatherland', the 'Motherland', 'kith and kin', are ideas which are political resources, and they have endured throughout the ages as objects of supreme emotion and loyalty. Wales is 'the Land of our Fathers'; Jews have traditionally defined themselves as descended from a Jewish mother, and the Law of Return of Israel allows Jews the right to live in the 'National Home of the Jewish People'; some Afrikaner nationalists formed themselves into a 'Brotherhood'; many British people felt sympathy for their 'kith and kin' in Rhodesia, despite their illegal 'Unilateral Declaration of Independence' in 1965, and for the (British) Falkland Islanders when they were invaded by Argentina in 1982. Citizens are expected to be ready to die for their 'Fatherland'/'Motherland', and it may even be natural to want to do so. One would hardly die willingly for one's job, one's social class, or even one's state, if that is not seen as the 'Fatherland'.

Why is this so? We can see that the rhetoric of nationalism draws heavily on the idea of the nation as a family, but is there any scientific reason why people should respond so strongly to such an appeal? We are born with genetic characteristics and instincts, and we cannot escape from them, although they can be cultivated in several directions. They are certainly the most primordial of human attributes, and apparently the most powerful. It is little wonder that such 'resources' are so easily and prominently tapped in politics. If there is a biological basis to nationalism and ethnicity it is easier to make sense of the kind of politics which results. Perhaps no other form of political activity is drawn so clearly from what some maintain are the biological 'givens' of human nature.

But how much politics is determined by biology? In the new field of 'sociobiology', scientists (natural and social) are engaged in fierce arguments, many of which are directly concerned with our subject (see for example, van den Berghe, 1981; Reynolds, Falger and Vine (eds), 1987; Shaw and Wong, 1989). The theories of 'inclusive fitness' and 'kin selection', most obviously appropriate to 'animal behaviour', can be brought to bear on human behaviour too. 'Inclusive fitness' is a theory in genetics first propounded by W. D. Hamilton in 1964. It has been summarised as follows: 'genes will spread if their carriers act to increase not only their own fitness or reproductive success but also that of other individuals carrying the same genes. A person's inclusive fitness is his or her personal fitness plus the increased fitness of relatives that he or she has in some way caused by his or her actions' (Reynolds *et al.*, 1987, p. xvii). The way to achieve 'inclusive fitness' is 'kin selection', or mating with relatives, and animal behaviour gives evidence for instinctive propensities to do this. 'Kin selection', however, is not the same as 'group selection', a much-disputed theory in biology. In 'kin selection' there is no hard-and-fast boundary involved between groups of mating individuals, as might be found between ethnic groups or nations. Rather, 'kin selection' is a consequence of 'gene selection' or 'individual selection', which gives rise to a 'mathematical probability' of mating and 'altruistic behaviour' among those most closely related to each other (Dawkins, 1989, pp. 7, 94). 'Group selection', on the other hand, would appear to relate more directly to ethnicity and nationalism, if ethnic groups and nations are the groups involved.

How much of this is relevant to politics? Potentially, a great deal, but at this stage in scientific theorising it is impossible to know how valid these theories are, even for non-human biology, since they are relatively new, and controversial. Nevertheless, these hypotheses are repeated here since they are part of the academic literature on nationalism and ethnicity. For this author, the balance of evidence seems to support the view that human nature includes instincts which are related to ethnocentrism and nationalist behaviour. For most social scientists, however, such ideas are anathema, since they seem to deny human freedom to escape from nationalist and racist prejudices and behaviour.

Even if the sociobiological approach is accepted, that does not imply any consensus regarding the effects of biology on political behaviour. In the collection of essays entitled *The Sociobiology of Ethnocentrism* (Reynolds *et al.*, *op. cit.*), the editors, after reviewing the biological explanations for ethnocentrism, reject the idea that selfishness and racism are 'genetic imperatives' of human nature (p. xv). Moreover, they state that 'There are no theoretical grounds for supposing that we cannot identify ourselves with humanity as a whole' (p. xix). But they also present biological evidence which points to instinctive behaviour, especially 'kin selection' among animals. Insofar as human beings are subject to 'animal behaviour', sociobiology must be taken seriously. Students of nationalism and ethnicity should be aware of the claims made by sociobiologists, and should test them against the evidence. So far, their theories do not amount to 'conventional science', especially with reference to human behaviour.

A more orthodox view than that of the sociobiologists is that human behaviour is the result of 'culture' and 'learning' rather than biology. If there is a biological component to ethnocentrism and nationalist behaviour, these writers argue, it is activated by society and politics, and can be suppressed or sublimated in the same way by these. But the evidence for that is as controversial as for the hypothesis that we are subject to our genes in this regard. Clearly, in human affairs there is an interaction between genes and environment, and neither is independent of the other.

The universal presence of ethnocentrism gives some support to the argument that it is genetically determined, but the form it has taken over the ages has varied considerably. It might even lie dormant politically in certain conditions. For example, the drive to reproduce one's genes through 'kin selection' may have little explanatory power in the conditions of a mobile and ethnically (genetically) mixed modern society. We may have few relations around us to mate with. But 'kin selection' instincts (if they exist) may still provide a 'necessary condition' for nationalist behaviour, xenophobia and ethnic/racial discrimination, even if the 'sufficient conditions' for such behaviour derive from political, social and economic circumstances. The biggest deficiency of sociobiological theories for the study of politics is that they are of little use in explaining why particular ethnic groups exist, and how nations were formed in history. So we have to move on to other types of theory if we are to understand fully the *politics* of nationalism and ethnicity.

Language is closely linked to ethnicity and nationalism, and it is also a facet of human nature. One political scientist (Laponce, 1985) has used certain 'neurophysiological and neuropsychological findings' to assert that there are physical reasons why particular languages are spoken by particular nations. He also suggests that unilingualism in a 'mother tongue' is more natural than bilingualism, for neuro-physiological and neuropsychological reasons. A dominant language, he says, will drive out a minority language in a bilingual or multi-lingual state, unless that state is divided into unilingual territories, as in Belgium and Switzerland. His conclusion for Quebec in Canada is that the French language there can only survive in a unilingual Quebec polity, since Canada as a whole is predominantly English-speaking. He thus supports the Quebec Nationalists and Liberals who seek a French-only-speaking Quebec.

Laponce is unusual in introducing a neurophysiological element into the discussion of language and nationalism, and as with the socio-biologists we are left wondering what scientific validity there is to his argument. One thing is clear. Whether the result of 'human nature' or not, language divisions are strongly related to ethnicity and nationalism, and we shall see in Chapter 2 that many 19th century nationalists based their ideology of nationalism on the claims of language communities to national independence.

Yet another way to approach human nature and its relationship with nationalism is through social psychology. Social psychologists have conducted experiments which have thrown light on how humans behave as members of groups. These experiments add to our understanding of the politics of nationalism and ethnicity.

In a well-known study of inter-group conflict and cooperation (She-rif, 1961), boys who were divided into two groups called 'the Rattlers' and 'the Eagles' soon developed hostility towards the opposite group, although there was no reason for their hostility. It seems that humans, when combined together in an 'ingroup', have a propensity for hostility towards members of an 'outgroup', especially if that group is clearly defined. They will also develop a sense of community with the other members of the 'ingroup', even where no other common attributes exist.

If this propensity for ingroup/outgroup hostility is given some sub-stance or supporting instinctive behaviour because of the ethnic char-acter of the groups, then the conflict is more serious. Suppose then that two groups are clearly defined as separate nations such as the English and the Scots, and people are firmly allocated to one or other of these nations. Since the idea of a nation is linked to kinship, even if the 'kin' are mainly distant relations or even 'fictive' kin (no real genetic relationship, but one that is believed to exist), we have in nationalism a combination of biological ethnocentrism, psychological ingroup/outgroup hostile propensities, and cultural and political differences. This makes it a special form of political behaviour and one which can be studied along with related forms of behaviour such as xenophobia, discrimination and racism (as in Reynolds *et al.*, *op. cit.*). Once again, however, the student of nationalism should be aware that although a 'human nature' or psychological approach looks promising, and may provide the necessary conditions for ethnocentrism and nationalism, the specification of the 'sufficient conditions' in any case requires an analysis of the nature of the groups and their conflicts. The distance between groups on a genetic and cultural scale is likely to exacerbate mutual ethnocentrism and nationalism. Conversely, similar groups will usually exhibit less hostility towards each other.

Groups may pursue goals of 'rational self-interest' leading to 'realistic group conflict', or they may display frustration or displacement leading to 'irrational ingroup-outgroup hostility' (LeVine and Campbell, 1972; Reynolds *et al.*, *op. cit.*). Depending on circumstances then, nationalism can be called either 'rational' or 'irrational'. Either way, it seems that it is firmly related to a human propensity to identify with an 'ingroup' and oppose an 'outgroup', once these are established and perceived. 'Boundary maintenance' is the aim of groups which feel threatened by other groups, and this applies to ethnic groups and nations too (Barth, 1969). They fight to preserve their territory, their language and their economic interests. So the activity of boundary maintenance in groups is paralleled in the nationalism of nations. However, Barth stresses that such groups are not 'givens', but the product of ever-changing situations.

An important political aspect is the perception of majority and minority status for national groups within the state. This gives a special psychological character to the ingroup-outgroup conflict. It is of course the state (or states) which provides the context for such a relationship. Thus, in Nigeria, the rhyme went:

I am a Hausa,	We are majorities,
Thou are an Ibo,	You are minorities,
He/she is a Yoruba.	They are different.

(quoted by Kirk-Greene, 1988, p. 159)

When the Nigerian federal structure made these identities highly political in the 1960s, civil war followed. Similarly, in Northern Ireland, the 'majority community' (Protestants/Unionists) faces the 'minority community' (Catholics/Nationalists) in endemic conflict. But here there is the added complication that in the context of a united Ireland, the Protestants become a minority group. Thus both Catholics and Protestants in Northern Ireland have psychological behaviour characteristic of minority groups.

Psychologists have paid particular attention to group 'stereotyping', and this is also a universal feature of ethnocentric or nationalist behaviour. 'Negative stereotyping' of foreigners gives substance to national identity in people's minds, and justifies national self-determination or sacrifices in wars against other nations. People of other nations are 'different', and usually threatening or inferior. In two world wars, British people called the Germans 'Huns', a barbarian tribe. In a more peaceful context, Scots often see English people as snobbish, and the Irish as lazy or irrational. That this may be the result of contacts in Scotland with particular English and Irish people is likely, and illustrates how stereotypes can be built up from unrepresentative samples.

Of course, all this is vague and general, and not necessarily very useful in explaining particular political situations. The biological and psychological characteristics of humans have not evolved greatly since the 'hunter-gatherer' society of several thousand years ago. Yet contemporary society is very different from that of prehistoric man. Today it is rare to find kin groups driven by instincts in a struggle for survival against the natural environment. Our society is the product of several thousand years of cultural and technological development, and is now highly mobile, and increasingly mixed genetically.

When we apply sociobiological theories to concrete examples in contemporary politics, their deficiences become apparent. Let us take nationalism in the United Kingdom. The ethnic (kin) groups which make up the present population of Britain are for the most part not easily defined biologically nor can they be readily recognised in physical appearance. Apart from the recent 'New Commonwealth' immigrants, who are well-defined and recognised because of their colour, the original ethnic groups such as the Picts, Britons, Celts, Angles, Saxons, and Danes, have largely merged in a larger ethnicity. The division between 'Scots', 'Welsh', 'English' and 'Irish' is only partly ethnic, either in biology (relatedness) or in psychology (perceived identity). There is certainly a core of ethnic distinctiveness present in these categories, but over the centuries inter-marriage has occurred quite widely, especially between the English and the Scots and the Welsh.

Moreover, 'identity' is only partly a spontaneous feeling which people have. It relates to the position they have in society, especially their membership of groups such as churches, which like nations can inspire emotion and supreme loyalties. When church and nation coincide, as they often do, the effect is to reinforce a sense of national identity. Thus the Scots and English each have their own national Church, presbyterian and episcopal respectively. Wales favours non-conformity, and the Republic of Ireland is almost entirely Roman Catholic. The Armenians' strong nationalism is linked to their identity as Christians in a Moslem environment. This religious difference, in a climate of Moslem fundamentalism, has led to their being the object of violence and even genocide. But their national identity is more than religious, since it is also made up of a language and consciousness of common descent. These indicators of nationality are not so marked in Scotland, England and Wales. Nevertheless, churches, and their related school system, have been powerful transmitters of nationality from one generation to the next in the nations of the British Isles.

Identity is partly imposed on people from outside their own group. Politics enters into this, since it is often the state which classifies people according to ethnic group, nationality and race. This may, or may not, be accepted entirely by the people concerned, but it usually leads to dual or multiple identities, especially when an historic national identity is overlaid with a contemporary political status such as citizenship, or with a new 'national' identification derived from the state (the 'official nation').

An example of this is the dual sense of national identity felt by most Scots and English people. Nearly all Scots feel a Scottish national identity, but most also feel British. This is because Scotland has been part of Great Britain since 1707, and there is a sense of identity with the state as well as with the Scottish nation. It is also true that the British state makes Scots conscious of their Scottish nationality. It does this by preserving a legal, political and administrative distinction between Scotland and England. Scots law, the Scottish Office, and Scottish education are powerful influences which make Scots Scottish and not English. English people, for their part, are made aware of being English by the state for some purposes (as in the Established Church of England), but for other purposes 'England' seems to mean 'Britain' (as in the Bank of England, the British state bank). It is little wonder then that English people are less sure than Scots of the difference between their historic nationality (English) and their modern citizenship (British). They often say 'English' or 'England' to mean 'British' and 'Britain', something that Scots cannot do with the terms 'Scottish' and 'Scotland'. Nevertheless, English people, like Scots, display dual national identity as 'English' and 'British', as for example in their loyalties to 'England' in football and to 'Britain' in international relations.

Similar situations are found in other parts of the world. 'Russians' identify with the USSR, and with their own 'nationality'. 'Yugoslavs' are a national category in Yugoslavia, and in 1981 1.2 million identified themselves as such, out of a total population of 22.4 million. In practice, most of these were of mixed ethnicity, in particular areas such as Bosnia, Croatia and Vojvodina. Under the Austro-Hungarian Empire (1867–1918), the identity 'Austrian' could cover any of the multitude of ethnicities in that state.

So 'national identity' is not a straightforward, exclusive concept. There are often 'dual identities', combining two 'national' identities, or more correctly one 'ethnonational' identity and one 'state' identity. In some places there may be more than two identities of this kind (e.g., Egyptian, Arab, Moslem), which may lead to conflicts of loyalty. In this book, the assumption is that the nation normally commands the 'supreme loyalty', but that may not be true in all cases.

Empirical evidence on national loyalties has been produced through surveys in several countries. Such a survey of Scottish national identity in 1986 found that 53% expressed a degree of 'dual nationality' and 45% 'single nationality'.

That these responses are to some extent politically determined is seen in the considerable variation in the responses according to which party is supported. Thus 58% of Scottish National Party supporters chose an exclusively Scottish identity, while only 27% of Conservative Party supporters did so. As nearly all (c. 90%) of the Scottish population is Scots-born, the different identities are not just a function of whether respondents were Scots-born or not. Rather they reflect the political connotations of national identity. Those choosing a 'dual identity' were likely expressing support for Scotland's membership of the United Kingdom, and those choosing only a Scottish identity were probably more inclined towards national self-determination for Scotland outside Britain.

That a sense of dual national identity is widespread is supported by research in other countries. In Catalonia for example, there is an even greater amount of dual Catalan/Spanish nationality (79%) than Scottish/British identity, despite the widespread use of the Catalan language and the success of Catalan nationalism in achieving devolution in 1979. 'Only Catalan' identity was 9%; 'more Catalan than Spanish' was 24%; 'as much Spanish as Catalan' was 47%; 'more Spanish than Catalan' was 7%; and 'only Spanish' was 12% (Moreno, p. 172).

When national identity is analysed as something ascribed to others, another useful perspective is gained. Again, Catalonia has been studied in this respect (Linz, in Tiryakian and Rogowski, 1985, p. 209). Now the question was 'Which of the following conditions are necessary, so that a person could consider himself a Catalan?' (the question was also asked of Basques, Galicians, and Valencians). The responses were then correlated with identities chosen by respondents for themselves.

It is interesting to see that, despite the strong linguistic character of Catalan national identity, only one-third consider the ability to speak Catalan to be a condition for someone to call himself a Catalan. An 'ethnic' criterion (Catalan descent/born in Catalonia) is strongly favoured, especially by those who state a Spanish identity, but a purely territorial criterion of 'living and working in Catalonia' is also given

Table 1.1 *Scottish national identity, 1986*

Q.   'We are interested to know how people living in Scotland see themselves in terms of nationality. Which of these statements best describes how you regard yourself?'

	Total	Party supported			
		Con	Lab	All	SNP
	%	%	%	%	%
Scottish, not British	39	27	37	34	58
More Scottish than British	30	29	35	26	29
Equally Scottish and British	19	22	20	28	7
More British than Scottish	4	10	2	3	3
British, not Scottish	6	10	4	7	2
Don't know	2	2	2	1	1

Source: Moreno, 1988, p. 171, quoting in part a *System Three Scotland* survey. Responses by party are taken from the original survey, not shown by Moreno.

Table 1.2   *Catalan national identification (1979)*

The proportion saying that a certain condition is necessary for someone to consider him/herself Catalan, by identity chosen of residents of Catalonia

	Condition		
Identity chosen	Live and work in Catalonia %	Speak Catalan %	Born in Catal., or descended from family %
Total	56.5	33.3	60.7
Spanish only	49.0	30.3	88.2
More Sp. than Catalan	64.9	32.7	89.2
As Span. as Catalan	60.5	34.5	81.9
More Cat. than Span.	64.1	45.5	71.8
Catalan only	51.5	27.0	77.2

Source: adapted from Linz, in Tiryakian and Rogowski, 1985, p. 209 (DATA survey).

by over half the respondents. Linz concludes (p. 250), from a comparison of Catalonia, the Spanish and French Basque countries, Galicia, and Valencia, that there is less 'primordial' nationalism based on language or descent in the regions of Spain than 'territorial' nationalism similar to that of the old 'nation-states', in which citizenship and nationality come together as national identity. These distinctions are similar to 'ethnic nationalism' on the one hand, and 'official nationalism' (as used in this book) on the other.

Similar features are found in Scottish nationalism. Scottish nationalists do not seek a 'Scotland for the Scots' or ethnic nation, but an independent government or state for Scotland. All who live and work in Scotland would be eligible for Scottish citizenship. This explains why some English people are Scottish nationalists.

It will be seen that we have moved some way from the biological and psychological discussion at the start of this chapter. We are now well into the complexities of modern national identity and political nationalism. What then is the place of human nature and the biological and psychological analysis of this subject?

Human nature and human psychology provide the 'necessary conditions' for ethnocentric and nationalist behaviour, and such behaviour is universal. As with all human behaviour, it is a result of the interaction of genes and environment. In experimental psychology, groups can be observed displaying hostility to one another in certain circumstances. This is similar to group ethnocentrism and nationalism, but these groups perceive an actual ethnic or national identity which gives an added force to their 'ingroup/outgroup' hostility.

We are not dealing with experiments however, but with real societies. In these the groups are usually less clearly defined, and identities may be confused and multiple. There is not often in politics a clear ingroup/outgroup distinction, and national identities are often dual or even triple. In a class of American students I taught, there were many definitions of personal national identity. One student wrote:

> Frequently, I am asked: 'What are you, really?' Everyone usually makes the general assumption that I am American but often feel they have to dig deeper.
>
> My mother is Italian from both sides of her family while my father is a Russian-Jew from his. I consider myself Italian mainly because almost all of my mother's family live in and around Pittsburgh. Along with my mother and father I feel that my mother's family was responsible for raising me. I have learned Italian culture, heritage and some language.
>
> Currently, I am studying the Italian language so I frequently do speak Italian with my grandmother who, luckily for me, does not speak a dialect.
>
> I will always be proud of my Italian heritage and try to pass on what I know to my children. As for my Russian heritage I still don't know much about it and no effort on my father's part to teach me has been made.

Identity and behaviour are partly genetic, but they are also shaped by context and choice. In politics they are resources waiting to be used by politicians and their supporters for their own advantage. Human nature provides the 'necessary' condition for ethnocentric behaviour, but politics converts this into the 'sufficient conditions' for nationalism as we understand it today.

2

Nationalism as Ideology

When people come to think about themselves and their position in society, their ideas are partly derived from their instincts (their nature), and partly from what they learn in their environment and from other people. Their *behaviour* is also in part instinctive, and in part the result of learning and environment.

'Nationalism' is both an ideology and a form of behaviour. It is of course in practice difficult to distinguish between the two, since the cause of the behaviour may in part be the ideology. As we have seen, 'ethnocentrism' and 'nationalist behaviour' is held by some to be partly instinctive. Giving it the name 'nationalist', rather than 'ethnocentric' focuses on the idea of the nation, and on the agenda which 'nationalism' sets for action relating to the nation. This idea and this agenda makes nationalism a special kind of ideology and behaviour, though it is closely related to ethnocentrism. While it is possible to examine nationalist ideology and behaviour separately from ethnocentrism, and from ideologies and behaviour such as racism, we cannot escape from the fact that we are in the same broad area of human activity.

The 'idea' of a nation can be considered as both natural and a product of the imagination. It is natural, if we accept the view of some sociobiologists, because it derives from the instinct of 'kin selection' or ethnocentrism discussed in the first chapter. In this view, a nation has the function of an extended family, whether or not it is genetically related – though it usually is, in a broad sense.

Most writers on nationalism see the nation as a concept rather than as something natural. To them, nations are 'Imagined Communities', in Benedict Anderson's phrase (Anderson, 1983). People imagine nations, and their membership of these, because their minds are trying to make social constructs out of their relationship with other people. Of course, this approach does not help us to determine which nations are 'imagined', and how strongly. Nor does it place nationalism in a historical context.

The idea of the nation and the idea of nationalism may be 'imagined' by many people with a minimum of prompting by political thinkers. But in its more developed form nationalism is an 'ideology', and this moves the focus from biology and psychology to sociology and philosophy. In these disciplines, an 'ideology' is usually seen as a system of ideas, different from 'knowledge' or 'science' because it is not 'true', and because it contains a great deal of special pleading. Nationalism is an ideology which builds on the idea of the nation and makes it the basis for action. This action can be political or non-political. As this book is about politics, it is not necessary to delve deeply into cultural nationalism, or nationalism in sport, unless these types of nationalism have clear political effects. The difficulty of knowing what is, and what is not, political is particularly puzzling in the study of nationalism.

For example, the most popular form of nationalist behaviour in many countries is in sport, where masses of people become highly emotional in support of their national team. But the same people may display no obvious nationalism in politics, such as supporting a nationalist party, or demanding home rule or national independence. Of course, most national teams represent states which have political independence, so their supporters' nationalism is 'official nationalism'. In Britain, however, there are four 'national' teams in international football: England, Scotland, Wales and Northern Ireland. This has led to some manifestations of 'social' or even 'ethnic' nationalism in a political form, as when Scottish supporters boo 'God Save the Queen' (the British, but also the English, national anthem), and sing their own unofficial anthems, 'Scotland the Brave' and 'Flower of Scotland', which are now played at international games. But Scottish football supporters do not seek political independence for Scotland more than other Scots, as far as is known, nor do they give massive support to the Scottish National Party. Yet a study of nationalism in politics cannot ignore such nationalist behaviour, because it underpins and heightens national consciousness, without which political nationalism would have no chance of success. Of course, the 'ideology' of nationalism involved here is minimal and is nearer to ethnocentrism than to political thought.

In the case of nationalism in sport we have three manifestations of nationalism: nationalist behaviour (perhaps biologically and psychologically derived – the 'animal behaviour' of the 'Soccer Tribe' (Morris, 1981)); a strong national consciousness (the 'imagined community' – the 'tribe' is now the nation and its object of emotion the national team); and an ideology of nationalism (the 'learned' sentiments of the national anthem with its patriotism and occasional xenophobia). These three components of nationalism recur time and time again in this study.

Where did the idea of a nation come from? And how did nationalism develop from that? These topics are the subject of much dispute among scholars, and in this work a particular interpretation will be given, which aims to be consistent with the rest of the argument. But other interpretations will be discussed which readers may find more convincing.

The idea of a nation is to be found as far back as the ancient world, although it is not clear that there was then what we understand as a nation today. Greeks and Jews in particular were conscious of their identity as peoples and acted to preserve their communities. In the case of the Jews, this was done throughout their prolonged 'diaspora' or dispersion throughout the world. While the Greeks retained their homeland, albeit under alien rule for many centuries, the Jews lost theirs until the twentieth century. The desire to return to the 'promised land' stayed with Jews throughout the centuries, and they repeated the prayer 'Next year in Jerusalem'. Zionism is the form of nationalism which in the late nineteenth century gave expression to this desire to rebuild a Jewish Homeland in Palestine. In 1917, the British Government in the Balfour Declaration promised to 'facilitate the establishment in Palestine of a national home for the Jewish people'. In 1948, the state of Israel was established, and in its declaration of independence it proclaimed 'the natural right of the Jewish people to be master of its own fate, like all other nations, in its own sovereign state'. The state of Israel would thereafter 'be open for Jewish immigration and for the ingathering of exiles'.

Here is an example of the idea of the nation and the ideology of nationalism existing over thousands of years, although taking a particular form (Zionism) only in the last hundred years. However, it should be pointed out that most writers take the view that nationalism is a relatively modern phenomenon, although having roots in the distant past (Kohn, 1944).

Not all nations are as clear-cut as the Greeks and the Jews. The historical record is very difficult to follow for most modern nations. What was a 'nation', or a 'people', or a 'race', at one period may disappear at another, or be merged with a larger community. Anthony Smith has come to the conclusion, after much study of nationalism, that nations have 'ethnic origins' (Smith, 1986). This means that we should not believe that nations have been produced only by modern developments, such as capitalism and industrialisation, as Gellner suggests (Gellner, 1983). Rather, they have origins in the ethnic groups of the earliest periods in history. This also pushes back the idea of the nation to the point where it was first expressed, rather than to the period when nationalist ideology was widely articulated ('the Age of Nationalism' in the nineteenth century).

We can see how this approach works when we look at the history of the Scottish nation. An early manifestation of national consciousness and nationalism is seen in the 'Declaration of Arbroath' of 1320. This was a letter sent by a group of Scottish nobles and others to the Pope, seeking his support for the independence of Scotland, which was being threatened by England. The letter asserts the idea of a Scottish nation, and propounds an ideology which equates national independence for Scotland with freedom for the national community, itself seen as a natural right. Similar statements about nationality and nationalism can be found in nearly all parts of the world, but there are few which have survived in documentary form from such an early period (for a discussion of the Declaration of Arbroath and its significance in Scottish history, see Duncan, 1970).

The Declaration of Arbroath starts with a list of signatories, who may be considered the articulators of the idea of the nation and of nationalism. They are the counterparts of the Scottish nationalists of today, although in the fourteenth century they were a select group of landowners and freeholders, rather than 'ordinary people' in a modern mass electorate. This is hardly surprising, as there was no such electorate in the fourteenth century. However, the function of articulating nationalism is performed by different people at different times, and even today only a minority of the Scottish nation is nationalist in the sense of articulating a nationalist ideology.

Much interest has been shown in the identity of nationalists: whether they come from a particular social class, whether they are intellectuals, and so on. It is not easy to get evidence for pre-modern periods, and the 1320 Declaration has been interpreted as the claim of 'a ruling elite group in defence of its property and privileges' rather than the claims of a nation-people to rule in some democratic way (Berry, 1981). Again, it is the difficulty of comparing modern nationalism with early nationalism that is involved here.

Nationalists are clearly idealists, since they propound the idea of the nation and the ideology of nationalism. They are also people with interests of their own to promote, whether it be feudal power in relation to a monarchy, or a material or psychic advantage as individuals or members of a group. So nationalist ideology is a justification for the pursuit of self-interest.

In some cases, nationalism verges on the irrational and may produce pathological behaviour. The study of 'the authoritarian personality' by Adorno and others (Adorno, 1950) linked personality traits with support for fascism. A later study of nationalism and personality (Forbes, 1985) has pointed out that the perception of differences between ethnic groups has more to do with the causes of nationalist behaviour than the personality characteristics of nationalists. So it seems that nationalism is not always peculiar or irrational behaviour but can be a rational response to particular circumstances, in this case the antagonistic interests of different nations. Even so, the excesses of nationalist (and xenophobic, racist, etc) behaviour do not show normal or rational activity in a civilised society, and it seems sensible to regard such behaviour as pathological. How personality and environment bring about such behaviour is not clear.

If we look at the 'ideas' and 'ideology' of the Scottish Declaration of Arbroath of 1320 we can see clearly how the ideology of nationalism is created, why, and by whom. The signatories were a narrow elite, but they claimed to speak for 'the whole community of the realm of Scotland', not just for a narrow group (even if that was what they were). Of course they did not seek democracy, rather independence for Scotland, and 'freedom': 'For we fight not for glory, nor riches, nor honours, but for freedom alone, which no good man gives up except with his life.'

How did they come to think of the idea of a Scottish nation at all? We know that the people of Scotland were made up of various ethnic groups, such as Picts, Britons, Angles, Norse . . . and Scots. The 'Scots' were only one group of incomers to north Britain (speaking geographically), but they ultimately (by the 11th century) gave their name to the Kingdom of Scotland, formed from a union of earlier kingdoms of the Picts, Scots, Britons, and Northumbrians (Angles).

The writers of the Declaration of Arbroath were not historians in any academic sense, yet they decided to describe the historical origins of the 'nation of Scots'. They thus first proclaimed a national identity and consciousness, something which is necessary for any nationalist ideology. Of course, this can be criticised as mere myth-making, not the truth. However, we are not concerned to discover what is true in nationalist ideas and ideology, but to point to the character of these ideas/ideology and their recurrence throughout history.

The nation of Scots, we are told, 'journeyed from Greater Scythia . . . dwelt for a long span of time in Spain . . . acquired, with many victories and untold efforts, the places which it now holds . . . In their kingdom one hundred and thirteen kings of their own royal stock have reigned, the line unbroken by a single foreigner'.

Here is the identity of a people, albeit constantly on the move, and only finally settling in a homeland after displacing or conquering 'Picts, Norwegians, Danes and English'. What clinches the nation's position is the kingdom, and its 'non-foreign' line (though the Scottish kings were never purely Scottish). So a political structure, the state, gives form to the idea of the nation, and the desire for a nation-state or for independence as an existing nation-state is the strongest form of political nationalism.

Once the nation of Scots is identified, with its political expression, the Kingdom of Scotland, these 1320 nationalists seek to endow the nation with good qualities, which are threatened by foreigners. This invokes the psychology of ingroup-outgroup tensions, as threats to a mythological extended family, the Scottish nation, are identified. The special qualities of the nation are already seen in its successes over other nations, on the path to political nationhood in Scotland: in this regard, 'among other distinguished nations our own nation, namely of Scots, has been marked by many distinctions'.

It was obvious at this time of pervasive religious culture that such a nation must be 'God's People'. Certainly, the Jews had already proclaimed their Covenant with God, which included a 'Promised Land' in Israel, and the Scots would also be expected to be appointed by God as a favoured nation. And so it is: 'Their high qualities and merits, if they were not otherwise manifest, shine out sufficiently from this: that the king of kings and lord of lords, our lord Jesus Christ, after his passion and resurrection, called them, even though settled in the uttermost ends of the earth, almost the first to his most holy faith.' This special relationship of the Scots to Jesus, would hopefully not be lost on the Pope, to whom the letter was addressed. 'God's People' is a favourite idea of nationalists, and apart from the Scots in the 14th century, Jews, Afrikaners and Mormons have used the phrase. It is a powerful reinforcement of the other foundations of subjective national identity.

When 'God's People' have a national church of their own this gives a strong institutional support to national identity and nationalism. Institutions tend to give rise to 'vested interests' which are social and economic as well as ideological. The Scottish nation is closely identified with the Church of Scotland, and even before the presbyterian Reformation the Christian Church was organised separately in Scotland. Thus the 1320 Declaration of Arbroath to the Pope sought national recognition for Scotland within the Roman Catholic Church as well as political independence for Scotland. This was to be granted by Rome. After the Reformation, the Church of Scotland was sharply differentiated from the Church of England within Protestantism because the former was presbyterian and Calvinist, while the latter was episcopalian and 'Anglo-Catholic' in theology.

There are many other examples of churches as sustainers of nationalism: the Armenian and Georgian Christian churches; Moslems in Punjab and Pakistan and Buddhists in Sri Lanka in opposition to Hindus; Catholics in Northern Ireland in opposition to Protestants; Catholics in Poland, Czechoslovakia and Hungary in opposition to Russian Communists and Orthodox Christians. Even where churches are international, as with Islam and Roman Catholicism, they usually display national characteristics in the context of different nations.

Nations unite to face a challenge from foreigners. In the fourteenth century, as before and since, the challenge to the Scots came from England, at the time of the Declaration of Arbroath from 'that mighty prince Edward, king of the English', whose 'wrongs, killings, violence, pillage, arson, imprisonment of prelates, burning down of monasteries, despoiling and killing of religious, and yet other innumerable outrages sparing neither age nor sex, religion nor order, no one could fully describe or fully understand unless experience had taught him'.

King Robert the Bruce managed to set the Scots free from these countless evils, 'Yet if he should give up what he has begun, seeking to make us or our kingdom subject to the King of England or to the English, we would strive at once to drive him out as our enemy . . . and we would make some other man who was able to defend us our king; for as long as a hundred of us remain alive, we will never on any conditions be subjected to the lordship of the English.' The Pope was asked to support the Scots' claim to independence in 'this poor little Scotland, beyond which there is no dwelling-place at all'. So the idea of the nation presumed the existence of a homeland, and no matter how humble or poor it was, the Scots sought to defend it from attack by the rich and powerful English. It is no surprise that even today Scottish nationalists refer with pride to the Declaration of Arbroath as an eloquent statement of Scottish nationalism and anti-English feeling.

Of course, the idea of the nation has developed over the centuries, even if its essence has not changed. During the French Revolution in the late eighteenth century, the nation took on a new political meaning which linked nationalism to the aim of popular sovereignty. This meant that the nation was no longer to be passive in the government of the state, but was to be an active participant, without which there would be no legitimate authority. The signatories of the 1320 Declaration of Arbroath could have no concept of participant popular sovereignty, even although they linked the legitimacy of the king to the defence of the nation. Modern Scottish nationalism breaks with the existing governmental and state structure, while the fourteenth century Scottish nationalists were defending their state and church from English attacks.

After the French Revolution nationalism became a revolutionary ideology, and the idea of the nation was for a time unsettling for most governments. The revolutionary aspect arose because the claim that the people were sovereign could not be accepted by the monarchs, aristocrats and merchants who ruled in nearly every state. Like democracy, this kind of nationalism was a political concept which sought to put all citizens on an equal footing, instead of excluding most from active membership of the state. It denied the legitimacy of a system of rule by social classes and status groups whose interests were not necessarily those of the whole nation. The idea of a nation now meant a community based on political equality and democracy, and democratic nationalism was the most powerful doctrine which spelled out why that was so, and how it was to be achieved.

As if that were not a big enough threat to the existing system of government, nationalism posed a second, equally disturbing, challenge to the state system. The idea of a nation was developed by some people along ethnic and linguistic lines, rather than according to democratic criteria. So while the revolutionary ideas of the French Revolution threatened monarchies and aristocracies in every state in Europe, ethnic and linguistic nationalists took this further and threatened the boundaries of states as well. This amounted to 'exclusive nationalism', since it excluded from the nation those people who were not ethnically or linguistically qualified to be members.

This involved a considerable amount of 'myth-making' about the historical credentials of the nation. Not every 'nation' in the Europe of the nineteenth century could point to a 'nationalist' document such as the Scottish Declaration of Arbroath, which had been drawn up in the fourteenth century. More common was an ideological construction by modern nationalists. Thus, Sabino Arana (1865–1903), 'had to invent a name, Euskadi, for the Basque country, design a flag for it, and construct an ideology which would justify the region's claim to independence from Spain' (Sullivan, 1988, p. 1). This ideology included a 'mythological' history of the Basque people and their descent from Noah. More complex were the nationalisms of the nations in present-day Yugoslavia (Banac, 1984). For example, according to Banac, the Slovenes 'acquired a national consciousness only in the nineteenth century and . . . the Montenegrins, Macedonians, and Bosnian-Hercegovinian Muslims . . . are the products of twentieth-century mutations in South Slavic national affinities and are, indeed, still in the process of formation' (Banac, 1984, p. 23). To Banac, the whole national problem in Yugoslavia can be seen as the product of competing and incompatible nationalist ideologies, some medieval and some modern. The older 'Greater Serbia' ideology threatens the modern nationalisms of Slovenia, Croatia, and Kosovo.

In the Third World, apparently 'primordial' identities are often in fact the product of comparatively recent developments. Thus, according to Greenberg (1980, pp. 14–15):

> The Kikuyu, for example, whose coherence is now so important to understanding Kenyatta and nationalism in Kenya, had no certain identity before the imposition of British rule and the alienation of land to the settlers; distinctive groups like the Sikhs in India, Ibo in Nigeria, and Malays in Malaysia were barely conscious of their 'sameness' one hundred years ago. Even race, seemingly universal and 'primordial', central to the entrenched group conflicts in southern Africa and the United States, only became a basis for broad group identity and ideology in the mid-nineteenth century.

Even revolutionary France came under nationalist attack by those who on ethnic or linguistic grounds did not consider themselves to be part of the 'French nation'. Orthodox French revolutionaries, however, defined the French nation in terms of the citizenship of the French state, which made no ethnic distinctions. Rather it resulted from the 'social contract' which all could make. This was to prove a continuing problem for France in an age of ethnic nationalism, for Corsicans, Bretons, and much later, Algerians and other 'non-French' colonials developed a non-French nationalism which would not rest content with citizenship of the French state. By the 1960s it also raised the question of whether Third World immigrants (especially Moslems) to France who did not share the French culture could be considered members of the French nation. By the late 1980s, this provoked a rise in anti-immigrant feeling, with strong voting for the National Front in cities such as Marseilles with a large immigrant population, and immigrants being attacked and even killed.

This is a problem for all states which are multiethnic in composition: that is nearly all the states of the world. Can 'equal citizenship' overcome ethnic and linguistic demands? If nationalism based on ethnicity and language is a powerful concept, how does the concept of a nation based on citizenship respond? An ideology of citizenship and the state which is not based on a single nationality can seek to establish a 'culturally plural' or 'multicultural' society, made up of several nationalities or ethnic groups each with the right to its own language, education, religion and so on. Or it can ignore these altogether and hope that the legitimacy of the state will be established through the support of all citizens without any recognition of minority ethnic and cultural rights. Only by achieving national homogeneity can such states hope to have much chance of success with this strategy, for it implies the assimilation (or at least integration) of minority ethnic groups to the majority national culture.

Once the idea of the nation and the ideology of nationalism became generally established in the political discourse of the world, they developed along lines which were to provide politics with its most powerful appeal to the emotions. Identity with a nation now appeared to be 'an inherent attribute of humanity', so that the idea of a man without a nation 'seems to impose too great a strain on the modern imagination' (Gellner, 1983, p. 6).

The 'Age of Nationalism' provides us with the classical statements of the nationalist ideology. Many of these texts have an archaic ring about them today, as well as a certain naivety. Nationalism never became a great system of ideas, as did liberalism or Marxism. But its influence on politics was even more important than these, if we look at the history of the modern world. Nearly all the wars of the nineteenth and twentieth centuries had their roots in nationalism, and all states now owe their legitimacy to some version of the national idea.

What is that idea? At its most abstract level, it seeks to place humanity in a context of time and place, rather than in terms of universal attributes. People belong to a particular nation, and are not 'cosmopolitan' or nation-less. Philosophically, this is the opposite of the Enlightenment view of people as the same everywhere at all times (Berry, 1981). Various writers propounded the idea of nationalism in different European countries during the nineteenth century, and their influence on nationalist movements was great. They are particularly famous in connection with German, Italian, and British nationalism, but their ideas spread to every part of the world, and inspired nationalists of all kinds.

Guiseppe Mazzini, the pioneer of Italian national unification, propounded the most exalted ideology of nationalism. For Mazzini, 'nationality' was closely related to the liberal principles of liberty and equality, but was especially concerned with fraternity. Unlike the atheism of the French Revolution, Mazzini's ideology was highly religious, as the following typical extract shows:

> We believe, therefore, in the Holy Alliance of the Peoples as being the vastest formula of association possible in our epoch; – in the *liberty* and *equality* of the peoples, without which no true association can exist; – in *nationality*, which is the *conscience* of the peoples, and which, by assigning to them their part in the work of association, their function in humanity, constitutes their mission upon earth, that is to say, their *individuality*; without which neither liberty nor equality are possible; – in the sacred *Fatherland*, cradle of nationality; altar and workshop of the individuals of which each people is composed. (Mazzini 1835, p. 47)

In this statement we can see an attempt to reconcile individualism, nationalism, and internationalism in one package with 'nationality' as the core organising principle. Mazzini distrusted what he called 'nationalism' as having a 'narrow spirit' (Mazzini, 1850, p. 5), because it neglected the overall association of nations. In Mazzini's scheme, nations are equal in status, though each has a particular character and function to perform in a world harmony of nations.

In Britain, this liberal view of nationality found an echo in John Stuart Mill's writings. In *Representative Government* (Mill, 1861), Mill proclaimed that 'Free institutions are next to impossible in a country made up of different nationalities. Among a people without fellow-feeling, especially if they read and speak different languages, the united public opinion, necessary to the working of representative government, cannot exist' (p. 361). It was this kind of thinking which led Victorian Britain to support nationalist movements in Europe, although it divided over that of Ireland. Mill himself was vague as to what constituted a nationality: his own Scotland is not mentioned, and the assumption was that Britain constituted a nationality, no doubt on the grounds of a common language.

German nationalist ideology also looked to language as the defining characteristic of the nation, but it had little of the liberalism of Italian and British national theorising. Johann Herder's writings predate the French Revolution (his major work on language and nationalism, *On the Origin of Language*, dates from 1772). Herder set the tone for German nationalism, which stressed the ethnic rather than democratic aspects of nationalism. The German *Volk* (people) is defined by its use of the German language, and the ancient origins of that language denote the ancient origins of the German folk or nation. Pride in one's language is a natural feeling, and is equally pride in one's nation.

> What a treasure language is when kinship groups grow into tribes and nations! Even the smallest of nations . . . cherishes in and through its language the history, the poetry and songs about the great deeds of its forefathers. (Herder, 1772, quoted in Barnard, 1969, p. 165)

Pride in one's nation and its language soon slides into assertions of national superiority, and Herder was particularly contemptuous of those Germans who used French instead of their native language (Edwards, 1985, p. 24). After Herder, a line of German nationalists developed the ideology of linguistic nationalism, and the superiority which the German language and literature gave to the German *Volk* (for example, Johann Fichte and Friedrich von Schlegel).

The political importance of these ideas was seen in the growing strength of nationalism in Europe in the nineteenth century. Nationalist movements took root everywhere, some directed towards national unification (Italy and Germany), some to throwing off the rule of multi-national Empires (Greece, Belgium, Poland, Hungary, Serbia), and some to breaking away from long-established kingdoms (Ireland, Norway). All these had their national ideologues and heroes, and they copied each other. For example, Mazzini's Young Italy society (1831) was imitated by other national liberation movements throughout Europe (notably the Young Turks of the early twentieth century), and later in Asia and Africa (Young India, Young China, Young Burma).

Of course, ideas catch on only in fertile ground. Ernest Gellner has asserted that the condition for the emergence of the national principle and nationalist movements was the stage of development reached in some states in Europe (Gellner, 1983). According to him, their emergence from feudalism into centralised state government and their change from agrarian/mercantile societies to industrialised economies gave nationalism its chance to become the politics of the progressive forces in Europe, and later in the rest of the world, where similar circumstances occurred.

What is not clearly explained in this analysis is how nationalism developed in conditions which were not those of the industrialising societies. Many European nationalist movements seem to have been inspired by the ideology of nationalism whatever the condition of the economy. The appeal of nationalist ideology was intellectual and emotional as well as functional in an economic sense. Its roots in ethnocentrism explain the emotional strength it possesses in politics, which no socioeconomic functional explanation is able to do.

The conditions favourable to the emergence of nationalism in its liberal forms (Mazzini and Mill) are not always present. Different conditions encourage other kinds of nationalist behaviour and different concepts of the nation. Pride in nation led to Fascism in Italy and Nazism in Germany in the 1920s. 'Social Darwinism' linked natural selection to nations, with the idea that some nations were 'fitter' than others. Spurious biology led to racism, with claims that some peoples were genetically superior, and entitled to rule over others. There were ideologies of 'white supremacy', especially in the South of the United States (racial segregation) and in South Africa (Apartheid), and an imperialist ideology of the 'White Man's Burden' in the British Empire. Almost everywhere there was anti-Semitism (an ancient attitude among Christians, but revived in the modern period, and linked to Nazism). The ramifications of such prejudices stretch into justifications for systems of slavery and castes, genocide, chauvinism and imperialism. Of course, there are differences between all these ideologies and the behaviour associated with them. Nationalism does **not** entail racism or genocide, but racism and genocide entail some form of nationalist ideology.

The idea of the nation and the ideology of nationalism at the simplest means the recognition of a people and its need for status, perhaps including its own state (the principle of 'national self-determination' was accepted in theory by American capitalists such as President Woodrow Wilson and by Soviet Communists such as Lenin and Stalin by 1917). Nationalism can take psychological, cultural or political forms: usually all three. Nationalist ideology can be left-wing, right-wing, constructive of new states or destructive of existing states. It can protect or destroy freedom, establish peace or lead to war. It is little wonder that it is difficult to tie down in political terms, and it is partly different in different periods of history. How historical change relates to nationalism is the subject of the next chapter.

3

The Evolution of Nationalism

For nationalism to emerge as a major force in politics, the conditions had to be right. These conditions may conveniently be divided into 'necessary' and 'sufficient' conditions. While ethnocentrism and an ideology of nationalism are both *necessary* for nationalist behaviour, the *sufficient* conditions for strong and widespread nationalism are more difficult to identify.

Writers on nationalism have provided us with a wide range of explanations for the rise of nationalism as a pervasive political force, and for the emergence of the nation-state as the most acceptable form of the state today. Writers on race and ethnicity have given us a related analysis of the conditions governing racial and ethnic politics. Case-studies of nationalist movements and ethnic politics provide a testing-ground for the hypothetical 'necessary' and 'sufficient' conditions for the emergence of nationalism and its political power in different contexts. In international relations too, nationalism comes up in various forms: as a cause of conflict; as a source of opposition to international or supranational institutions and cooperation; and as a determinant of a state's power. The conditions which strengthen nationalism in domestic politics may also strengthen it in international politics. At the same time, international circumstances have a strong effect on nationalism within states.

In the succeeding chapters, each of these subjects will be examined, and they all point to the general problem that historical change and different contexts in the contemporary world are exceedingly complex to study, and are the subject of widely divergent analyses. In some cases, these analyses have the character of general systems of thought or ideologies, as for example, Marxism, and 'universalist' or 'individualist' liberal thought. Both of these attack nationalism and seek to eliminate the context in which it thrives. Moreover, there is a fundamental difference between 'primordialists', who trace nationalism back to instinctive behaviour and the earliest societies, and 'context-ualists' who see nationalism as the product of particular economic and social circumstances, especially those of modern times (a useful survey of both types of theory is found in *Theories of Race and Ethnic Relations*, edited by John Rex and David Mason (1986)). Leaving aside the controversial 'primordial' type of theory, we can now go on to look further at the contextual conditions in which nationalism as we understand it developed from ethnocentrism, and ethnicity became nationhood.

This requires us to focus on three distinct, though related, facets of society: politics, economics and culture. Politics is essentially about power and authority. We are especially interested in the nature of 'the polity' (the state, principality, clan, etc), and how it relates to 'the nation'. The focus on economics concerns the pursuit of wealth and how the economy divides people into occupational classes. Are there economic explanations for nationalism?

Culture is about identity and status in terms of birth, family, language, religion, and so on. Ethnicity and nationalism are usually considered to be more clearly related to culture than to anything else, but most theories of nationalism seek to determine the particular relationship between politics, economics and culture which brings about the transition from ethnicity to nationalism. Table 3.1 summarises one way of analysing this relationship, which is similar to that of Gellner.

The table indicates that we can look for an explanation for the rise of nationalism in the developments which have taken place in politics,

Table 3.1 *Politics, the Economy, and Culture and nationalism*

Period of History	**Politics** power/ authority	**The Economy** wealth/occ- upation/class	**Culture** identity/status, language, etc
Pre-nationalist	The pre-modern polity	The pre-indus-trial economy	'Primordial' ethnicity
Nationalist	The modern state	The industrial economy	Nationalism

in the economy, and in culture. The interactions between these three dimensions, at different periods of history, provide the key to the understanding of nations and nationalism.

For some theorists, these interactions are structured in such a way as to make one part (represented in the table by one column) dominant, as the ultimate 'reality' in the analysis. For example, Marxists and other economic determinists believe that social and political behaviour can be reduced to economic interests, particularly those of economic classes, sections, groups, etc. Thus nationalism is seen as either a disguised economic interest, or in Marxist terms as 'false consciousness' which has misled people and stopped them pursuing their 'true' class interest.

Other 'reductionists' choose political power as their 'reality'. They see politics and the state as the producer of nations and nationalism. Economic and cultural identities and interests are ultimately subsumed under the primacy of political power (for this approach, see Breuilly, 1982, and Brass, 1985).

Nationalists, and some theorists of nationalism, are also 'reductionists'. For them, individuals, the state, and the economy are all ultimately dependent on membership of a particular nation. Where individualists seek to study the rights and duties of individual citizens in relation to the state, nationalists and some theorists of nationalism are concerned with the composition of the state rather than with the relationship between the state (any state) and the individual. They thus pose a prior question – 'What is my state?' – before those posed by most political theorists. Before discussing rights and duties, etc, of citizens, and the legitimate powers of the state, nationalists want to know what body of citizens, in terms of birth and culture, makes up the legitimate composition of the state.

Behind the discussion of the relationship between politics, economics and culture there is a time factor. Contextualists assert that there was a 'pre-nationalist' period in which the relationships between politics, economy and culture were not conducive to nationalism. This was followed by a nationalist period, in which they were. In the 'pre-nationalist' period, and in places today which share the conditions prevalent in that period, the 'state' had not achieved its modern form of a centralised, sovereign and bureaucratic polity. Rather, it was a loose collection of sovereignties or power centres, as in feudalism or tribalism. The economy was agrarian or pre-industrial, and nationalism was found only as ethnocentrism, or as loyalty to clan chiefs, kings and princes.

To enter the period of nations and nationalism, with a world based on the legitimacy of 'nation-states', all three dimensions of politics, economics, and culture had to be transformed. Thus the polity had to become a centralised state, the economy had to be modern not feudal, and the culture had to replace ethnicity with something which can become nationhood.

This kind of account can be found in many theories of nationalism, especially that of Gellner (for a short monograph also on this theme, see Berki, 1986). It is typical of Marxist studies of the emergence of nationalism, and in later variations of Marxism such as the theory of 'internal colonialism', discussed below. These combine an analysis of economic conflicts in capitalist states with an explanation for nationalism. Marxists look especially at how nationalism affects different socioeconomic classes. Greenberg, whilst distancing himself from Marxist analysis and 'modernisation' theory, nevertheless concludes that 'identifiable forces in capitalist development carry forward and elaborate patterns of racial and ethnic domination' (Greenberg, 1980, p. 405). For him, 'Racial domination . . . is essentially a class phenomenon' (p. 406), and racist and nationalist ideology is to be explained mainly in terms of class interests, in particular, those of (white) commercial farmers, businessmen, and industrial workers. These interests, however, are always changing, and may turn against racism and nationalism, although there is no universal process of 'modernisation' which decrees that they will inevitably do so.

The transition from ethnicity to nationalism is represented in the third column of the table, that dealing with culture. Some theorists see this process as a fairly self-contained cultural process (they are 'reductionists' in favour of culture). For them, nationalism develops from ethnicity through the articulation of the idea of the nation and the ideology of nationalism, and the rise of a national culture in a printed language, literature, national religion and education, etc. Other theorists, who still stress the primacy of culture, see the process as related to developments in the polity and the economy. They point out that at first the role of the state was so weak that ethnic groups lived in virtual isolation from each other in an economy which was mostly agrarian and localised. As kingdoms expanded their territories, ethnic groups were united under one ruler, and the economy developed, with more trading across ethnic boundaries. In this context, the members of different ethnic groups developed a common culture, which made them into a 'nation'. This culture typically consisted of a language, a religion, education, and folk arts. For Karl Deutsch, a people or nation is 'a community of social communication' based on a common culture (Deutsch, 1966). In a more developed polity and economy this became a 'high culture', with universities, art, literature, and music. Such was the cultural nature of the transition from ethnicity to nationhood.

While nations have their origins in ethnic groups, it is not easy to determine exactly how or when they arose. The prevailing view is that nations came about in the modern age because of a special combination of political, economic and cultural processes and events. There are many theories which explain the emergence of nationalism in the modern world, and well-known recent ones are by Karl Deutsch, Michael Hechter, Stein Rokkan, Ernest Gellner, Benedict Anderson, and Anthony Smith. These are chosen because of their importance, and because they illustrate some of the arguments discussed above. A short summary of each of these theories is provided, as well as an opinion as to its merits and drawbacks. Of course, the reader will have to make up his or her own mind in the light of the discussion as to which is the most convincing theory.

There are many other theories about the emergence of nationalism in the modern world, in particular those based on Marxism (for an account of some of these theories of nationalism, see Smith, 1983). Marxist theory and practice relating to nationalism will be dealt with later, in the context of nationalist movements in communist states. The theories chosen here are representative of the thinking outside Marxism and the last four appeared as recently as the 1980s, even if some of their conclusions are found in the writings of earlier authors.

Deutsch's Theory of Nationalism

Karl Deutsch, the American political scientist, wrote *Nationalism and Social Communication: An Inquiry into the Foundations of Nationality* in 1953, with a 2nd edition in 1966. It has become a classic in the study of nationalism, although it has its critics (e.g., Smith, 1983, p. 100), and it has not had many imitators in subsequent writings on the subject.

Deutsch was unusual in seeking to quantify and measure the elements of nationality, looking particularly at 'social communication' (common language and interpersonal transactions of all kinds). A people or nation is defined by the 'complementarity or relative efficiency of communication among individuals' (p. 188). Behind the reasoning of this theory was the then-fashionable 'systems theory' derived from cybernetics, with its measurement and use of 'messages' which sustain a system. Deutsch also represents the school of thought which sees nations and nationalism as the product of 'modernisation' – the

> social mobilisation which accompanies the growth of markets, indus-
> tries, and towns, and eventually of literacy and mass communication.
> The trends in this underlying process of social mobilization could
> do much to decide whether existing national trends in particular
> countries would be continued or reversed. (*loc. cit.*)

As Deutsch admits, 'this is largely a book on research and methods of research' rather than on nationalist movements. But it attracted attention to the basis of the nation as being a pattern of transactions which marked it off from other nations, thus broadening the focus from language to all kinds of social and economic data. It also asserted 'modernisation' theory, which was to prove so popular in the 1960s and 1970s, but which is now largely discredited.

When one looks at how particular examples of nationalism are treated by Deutsch, one sees the difficulty of relating such data to political movements. Thus, while Deutsch correctly plots the decline of the Gaelic-speaking and agricultural population of Scotland, he entirely fails to relate this convincingly to Scottish nationalism, which was based on other considerations. Nevertheless, an analysis of communication networks in Scotland, marking it off from England, would have been a good way to measure the functioning of the Scottish political system and its potentiality for nationalism.

Hechter's Theory of 'Internal Colonialism'

Michael Hechter's *Internal Colonialism. The Celtic fringe in British national development, 1536–1966* (Hechter, 1975) is another land-mark contribution to the study of nationalism, especially in the British context. Hechter, an American, was, like Deutsch, attracted to the research methodology of providing quantitative evidence to support his thesis. He was also influenced by 'modernisation theory' or 'diffusion theory' which, like that of Deutsch, posits the view that 'from inter-action will come commonality' and ethnic homogenisation (Hechter, p. 7).

Hechter, however, reacted against diffusion theory, and posited instead 'internal colonialism'. He maintained that modernisation and increased contact between ethnic groups within a state will not necessarily bring about ethnic unity, but will be just as likely to lead to ethnic conflict. This is because the inequalities between the regions in a country will relegate peripheral regions to an inferior position, leaving the core region dominant. The reaction to this in the peripheral regions will be hostility to the core, and if these regions are also national in character, this will take the form of nationalism. Thus Hechter saw Scottish, Welsh and Irish nationalism as the result of 'internal colonialism' by the English core.

Hechter's book was published before the rise of Scottish and Welsh nationalism in the late 1960s, but he has published since on the subject (Hechter, 1985). The principal change between the two publications is in the nature of his 'cultural division of labour' theory. This theory states that in a situation of internal colonialism, there will be a social stratification of ethnic or cultural groups, with the core group occupying the best class positions and the peripheral groups the inferior positions. This corresponds to a 'colonising' nation and 'colonised' nations. Thus, in Britain the English are the colonisers, and the Scots, Welsh and Irish the colonised.

Unfortunately for this theory, the facts seem to be at variance with such a division of labour. For example, Scots are not in practice relegated to inferior social positions in Britain, and Scotland has been as much an industrialised and imperial nation as England from the eighteenth century. This is not to say that there are not important regional inequalities in Britain, due to 'uneven economic development' and to government and commercial policies favouring the south of England. All these have contributed to a rise in nationalism in Scotland and Wales.

Hechter took account of the criticisms levied at his theory (e.g., Page, 1978; Greenberg, 1980; Brand, 1985) and revised the 'cultural division of labour' thesis (a hierarchical stratification) as regards Scotland to a 'segmental cultural division of labour' (a vertical stratification) in which Scots occupy 'occupational niches' deriving from the distinctiveness of their national institutions, such as law and education. These may not be inferior positions to those found in England, since they include high class occupations. So the group solidarity of 'colonised' nations and their assumed conflict with the colonisers is now called into doubt. By 1985 Hechter saw the capacity of nationalist organisations to attract support as being as important as the structure of internal colonialism (Hechter, 1985, p. 25). Nevertheless, his model remains a compelling one in many contexts (if not clearly in Scotland), and it will be returned to in the context of nationalisms in many parts of the world. The recurrence of a 'cultural division of labour' in most multiethnic societies is particularly striking.

Rokkan's Theory of Regionalism

While not strictly a theory of nationalism, Stein Rokkan's work on regionalism in Europe with Derek Urwin (Rokkan and Urwin, 1982; 1983) is relevant to 'nation-building' and the problems of core–periphery relationships. It also deals extensively with 'the politicisation of peripheral predicaments' and 'the central response'.

Rejecting the 'diffusion' model of Deutsch, but not endorsing the 'internal colonial' model of Hechter, Rokkan and Urwin conclude that:

> there is no simple centre–periphery polarity across culture, economics and politics. Peripheral predicaments and politicisation emerge out of the incongruity between cultural, economic and political roles, an incongruity which has existed on the continent as long as there have been states. While this remains unresolved, the potential for territorial problems remains, irrespective of the waxing and waning of individual parties or movements. (Rokkan and Urwin, 1983, p. 192)

It appears then, that it is a matter of degree whether the 'incongruity between cultural, economic and political roles' will lead to nationalism in particular situations. Rokkan has shown that students of nationalism ought to measure the degree of harmony between such roles in a state. They should then be able to predict that a strong mismatch between these roles will lead to nationalism.

Gellner's Theory of Nationalism

Ernest Gellner's *Nations and Nationalism* (Gellner, 1983) represents a type of theory which stresses the primacy of material conditions in shaping political thought and social change. In this it resembles Marxism, which Gellner nevertheless disavows. He proposes a fundamentally economic reason for the rise of nationalism. This is the development of 'industrial society', which took place in certain parts of Europe at the end of the 18th century, and then during the 19th and 20th centuries throughout most of the world.

The connection between nationalism and industrialisation is that particular forms of polity and culture are required if industrial economic growth is to occur. These forms combine in the nation-state. Once industrialisation took off, the old states were generally unable to maximise their advantages and profits until they changed both their cultural life and their state structure.

In place of the feudal or agrarian society, with its diversity of languages, cultures and ethnic groups, there had to be a homogeneous society with an educational system for all. This education would train workers and managers for industry, and provide all with a common 'high culture'. It was necessary to have one common language in a modern industrial society, for the mobility and division of labour would come from that, and from the education which all received.

Gellner, unlike many other writers on nationalism, does not believe that nationalism happened because some European thinkers invented it and forced it on political systems which would have been better off without it. Rather, he believes that nationalism 'has very deep roots in our shared current condition, is not at all contingent, and will not easily be denied' (*ibid.*, p. 56). This means that nationalism achieved its successes because it was appropriate for the needs of the time, rather than as an ideology which could be accepted or rejected intellectually in competition with other ideologies.

At this point, attention focuses on another 'necessary condition' for nationalism, the changing structure of the state. The medieval European state was unsuited to the task which industrialisation demanded. It was generally weak at the centre, preferring to operate through semi-independent aristocrats and churches. While some monarchies, such as those of England, France, and Prussia, began to reduce the power of the barons and the church in the name of royal 'sovereignty', there was little attempt to achieve a uniform culture within these countries. Indeed, several languages continued to be spoken in most countries, and often the king himself was imported from a foreign land. George I of Great Britain, for example, came to the throne in 1714 from Hanover in Germany, and spoke German, not English. There was little public education, and most education went to aspiring churchmen, lawyers, and landowners. This was often in Latin, a non-vernacular and pretty useless language as far as economic and social change was concerned. Only with a state education system in the vernacular, geared to the needs of industry, could progress be made. This meant a strong, centralised state, and a population free to work where it wished, without barriers of a feudal, religious, or linguistic nature.

The breakdown of the feudal state, and the emergence of centralised 'sovereign' authority was important for the development of nationalism, for it provided a strong state structure from which a homogeneous nation could be shaped. Control by the political authority from the centre over education, religion and law, swept away many local cultures or ethnicities, and replaced them with one large nation. In this way, 'nation-states' emerged. Where these were not formed, and the principle of 'one state, one culture' was denied, there was nationalist activity. While this theory applies particularly to the historic development of nationalism in Europe, it has clear relevance to new states (especially in the Third World) which are not 'nation-states' in the sense defined by Gellner.

Gellner's theory is compelling, but it has its limitations. There is little here about the primordial roots of nationalism, and its powerful emotional appeal. Why should people be prepared to die for what is in this analysis an imperative of a rational economic and social system of industrialisation? Nationalist behaviour in its contemporary form is hardly explained in this theory. It deals instead with the reasons why industrialising states adopted a national form in order to prosper, and the nationalism which was associated with that.

At one point, Gellner does address the question of the sharpness of nationalist conflict, but he relies again on a socioeconomic explanation. In the early industrial age, he says, wide social chasms and the uneven diffusion of industrialisation produced social conflicts, especially when cultural (ie, national) differences marked off these chasms. When cultural differences did not correspond to class divisions, 'nothing much happened' (p. 121).

> Classes, however oppressed and exploited, did not overturn the political system when they could not define themselves 'ethnically'. Only when a nation became a class, a visible and unequally distributed category in an otherwise mobile system, did it become politically conscious and activist. Only when a class happened to be (more or less) a 'nation' did it turn from being a class-in-itself into a class-for-itself, or a nation-for-itself. Neither nations nor classes seem to be political catalysts: only nation-classes or class-nations are such. (*ibid.*)

In this rather obscure passage, Gellner attempts to reconcile class analysis with nationalism, something which Marxists also seek to do. The main difference between Gellner's theory and that of most Marxists is that Gellner sees nationalism as the concomitant of any type of industrialisation, while most Marxists make nationalism dependent on capitalism as such. With the arrival of proletarian rule, according to Marx, nationalism becomes redundant. Gellner, on the other hand, does not see any future situation without nationalism.

Gellner's discussion of the matching of class and national divisions has a clear parallel in Hechter's theory of internal colonialism, with its 'cultural division of labour'. But in his desire to establish the 'nation-state' as the norm for modern society, Gellner has to reject 'multicultural society'. For him, a homogeneous culture, at least at the level of 'high culture' is necessary for modern states, although there may be room for innocuous folk cultures 'in a token and cellophane-packaged form' (p. 121). There is no place in his theory for cultural pluralism and 'consociational democracy', which tries to combine different national cultures within one state (see Chapter 9).

We can accept much of Gellner's historical analysis of how nation-states and nationalism emerged strongly at the time of industrialisation in Europe, when the breakdown of feudalism had taken place. It is more difficult to find in Gellner an explanation for the emergence of nationalism in pre-industrial times (e.g. Scotland in the Middle Ages, or England in Elizabethan times), and in non-industrialised countries in the Third World. Moreover, nationalism arising out of 'post-materialist values' in 'post-industrial' societies (Inglehart, 1977) is clearly different from nationalism resulting from industrialisation. In all these contexts the conditions are different from those in 19th century 'nationalist' Europe. Many nationalisms are found in countries which are largely agrarian, non-industrialised, and non-centralised. A very important determinant of nationalism in the Third World is the legacy of colonialism, and the independence movements directed against 'White Rule'. Contemporary nationalisms have arisen in long-industrialised countries such as Britain, Belgium, and Spain, which Gellner might have called 'nation-states'. Something new seems to have happened there, outside Gellner's theory.

Nevertheless, Gellner's short book is a masterly study of the emergence of nationalism in history, and is a yardstick with which we can measure other writings on nationalism. It does not tell us all we want to know, but it gives us a clear theory relating nationalism to industrialisation, 'high culture', and the structure of the modern state.

Benedict Anderson's Theory

Benedict Anderson's book, *Imagined Communities. Reflections on the Origin and Spread of Nationalism* (Anderson, 1983), is another recent major contribution to the study of the evolution of nationalism.

Unlike Gellner, Anderson is concerned to explore the psychological appeal of nationalism: 'What makes people love and die for nations, as well as hate and kill in their name?' (*op. cit.*, dustjacket). Obviously, a purely functional approach such as Gellner's will not explain the emotions engendered by nationalism, yet Anderson does not go to the other extreme of a sociobiological or primordial interpretation. He takes a historical, rather than a timeless, universalist approach, so that nationalism is seen to emerge at a specific period in European history. Anderson's originality lies in his explanation of how and why people in certain circumstances come to 'imagine' themselves part of a nation, and why such an 'imagined community' has such a powerful attraction for them.

He first builds up a set of necessary conditions for the emergence of nationalism. These are partly material, and partly psychic. More subtly, he analyses the 'pilgrimages' which people make in their social and economic lives. It is these pilgrimages which define the boundaries of the nation, and lead people to identify with it and not with another social or political entity. Such pilgrimages may thus be taken to be the sufficient condition for particular nations to be 'imagined' and form the focus of nationalism. This seems to be a combination of Deutsch's community of communication, and Hechter's 'cultural division of labour'.

The principal material precondition for nationalism, according to Anderson, is what he calls 'print-capitalism', meaning commercial printing on a widespread scale. It is this which spreads the idea of the nation and the ideology of nationalism, not only within one 'nation', but throughout the world. Through print-capitalism, vernacular languages are strengthened by the publishing of dictionaries and literature generally. In this way, nations are 'imagined' by many people, and linguistic nationalisms take root.

Printing standardises languages, and also aids the development of capitalism and the centralised state. A sense of nationality flows from the common language and education which printing facilitates. But the emergence of nationalism also depended on some other 'modernising' processes, such as scientific discoveries and the exploration of the world. These broke down old ways of looking at society, and also broke the unity of Christendom and the Moslem world, with their associated international languages, Latin and Arabic. The monarchical state too, with its 'divine right of kings' and hierarchical authority structure, gradually gave way to rule 'by the people'.

At this point, Anderson links up with Gellner's theory, which connects nationalism with modernisation and the needs of the industrial state. But he goes further than Gellner by explaining the emotional power of nationalism. He draws attention to nationalism's appeal as a faith in an everlasting life through membership of a continuing nation. The nation represents the continuity of the extended family from one generation to the next. In an age of declining religion, with its belief in an after-life, nationalism has a special appeal as a 'secular transformation of fatality into continuity, contingency into meaning' (p. 19). Anderson stresses the character of nationalism, not as a political ideology self-consciously followed, but as a cultural system with religious characteristics.

By pursuing the notion of 'pilgrimages' – essentially the pattern of social communication and 'life chances' of different peoples – Anderson is able to explain why nationalism has been found in every type of society in the modern world. The nation is often the social grouping which represents the boundary for mobility, both geographic and economic. This may be a matter of sharing a common language, or of being the object of differential treatment by the state. If an individual is identified as the member of a particular nation, this may give access to power and wealth, or conversely, discrimination and deprivation.

In the first instance, it is the state which determines which 'pilgrimages' can be made by members of different nations within it. Indeed, the state may decide who the members of the nations are. It does this to protect the interests of the powerful, and to keep other groups in a subordinate position. This is not necessarily anything to do with industrialisation (as in Gellner's theory), but is much more about political and social power generally. (For an extended treatment of the role of the state in shaping nationalism and the character of ethnicity, see Paul Brass (ed.), *Ethnic Groups and the State*, 1985.)

This means that the development of nationalism can be analysed in almost any society, and not just in industrial society. For wherever a system of status and power divisions is based on nationality, nationalism is likely to flourish. This was the case in the multinational Empires of Europe, and in the European colonies in America, Asia, and Africa. In these areas, the imperial system confined the life chances or 'pilgrimages' of natives (including Europeans born there, known as 'creoles' in Latin America) to the colonies. Eventually, these natives saw themselves as members of a nation in rebellion against the imperial country. In this way, nationalism was born in the colonies. It was led by two groups, called by Anderson, 'pilgrim creole functionaries and provincial creole printmen'. The former were administrators and businessmen of native or creole origins, and the latter native/creole intellectuals and writers whose publications inspired national consciousness. Because of the policies of imperialism, they were cut off from advancement in the imperial home country and followed their 'pilgrimages' or careers in the colonies, which they came to perceive as separate nations in rebellion against the imperial country.

A later refinement of the concept of 'pilgrimages' relates to 'official nationalism', which reacts against the new vernacular (in this book 'social' or 'ethnic') nationalisms. Fearing the breakup of the state through nationalist separatism, the old dynastic states begin a nationalism of their own. They try to impose a particular national culture on the whole state, and make that the condition for advancement, socially, politically and economically. Thus, the Russian Empire of the Czars instituted the policy of 'Russification', making the use of the Russian language obligatory throughout the Empire (this policy was also followed by the communists in the USSR). In the ex-colonies in Africa and Asia which gained independence after 1950, similar official nationalisms can be found, linking successful 'pilgrimages' in their societies to the adoption of a national language and culture sponsored by the state.

The title *Imagined Communities* points to the mental processes involved in nationalism. Members of even the smallest nation can never know most of their fellow nationals, 'yet in the minds of each lives the image of their communion' (p. 15). This is not a question of 'false consciousness', for there are, Anderson says, no 'true' communities larger than face-to-face primordial villages. All other communities are imagined.

Anderson introduces new perspectives into the study of how nationalism has evolved. But there is ambiguity in his conditions for the emergence of nationalism. Printing could destroy nations as well as create them. Many languages and nations (or ethnic groups) have died or been weakened in competition with literary languages and nations possessing printing resources.

As for religion, it seems that it is not always replaced by nationalism, but may go hand-in-hand with it. We have seen that churches have reinforced nationalism in such countries as Ireland, Poland, Armenia, Israel, and Iran. It is difficult therefore, to relate the rise of nationalism to the decline of religion, except perhaps in some mainly materialist societies. In some cases, religion and nationalism thrive together; in others, where a church is strongly supranational (as the Roman Catholic Church, or Islam), there may be tension between loyalty to religion and loyalty to the state or nation. However, even supranational churches can underpin nationalist movements against oppressive states which deny nationalism its free expression. Thus the Roman Catholic Church and Islam are closely involved with nationalism in Eastern Europe and Asia.

Anderson's use of the idea of 'pilgrimages', points to the pattern of communication and social mobility as a powerful binding force in the consciousness and action of social groups (as Karl Deutsch did earlier). But there seems to be a prior question here: why do ethnic or national groups crop up so often in social stratification? Why do people seem to prefer their fellow nationals as companions on their pilgrimages, and why do states use nationality as a method of dividing power? Can there be something special about nationality which is not present in other social, economic and political divisions? Our final theorist, Anthony Smith, focuses on this in the ethnic origins of nationalism, and its special characteristics.

Anthony Smith's Theory of Nationalism

Anthony D. Smith's book, *The Ethnic Origins of Nations* (1986) focuses on ethnicity as the precursor of nationalism, and gives an explanation of the transition from ethnic identities and loyalties to those relating to nations. For Smith, 'modern nations simply extend, deepen and streamline the ways in which members of *ethnie* [Smith's term for ethnic groups] associated and communicated. They do not introduce startlingly novel elements, or change the goals of human association and communication' (p. 215).

He is thus concerned to emphasise the continuity between ethnic identities and loyalties on the one hand and nationhood and nationalism on the other. In contrast, both Gellner and Anderson stress the essential *novelty* and *modernity* of nationalism. Smith does acknowledge the changes which made ethnicity into nationalism, and his explanations are similar to Gellner's and Anderson's. For example, the decline of religion, the rise of the centralised and bureaucratic state, as well as the pressures of the industrial economy are necessary for 'ethnie' to be mobilised and politicised into nations. But the 'new imaginings' and new thoughts (clearly a reference to Anderson's *Imagined Communities*) which lead people into national consciousness and nationalism are not really so new. Their essence can be found in pre-national communities at least as far back as Ancient Greece and Rome, although there was an ambivalence at that time about 'the masses' and their claim to be included in the 'ethnie'. Apart from this, Smith concludes,

> it is clear that modern nations and nationalism have only extended and deepened the meanings and scope of older ethnic concepts and structures. Nationalism has certainly universalized these structures and ideals, but modern 'civic' nations have not in practice really transcended ethnicity or national sentiments . . . In terms of ends, as opposed to means, there is a remarkable continuity between nations and *ethnie*, nationalism and ethnicism; continuity but not identity. (p. 216)

Smith moves the study of nationalism back to the pre-modern period, as Hans Kohn did in *The Idea of Nationalism* (1944). But Smith sees more in common between modern nations and their precursors than Kohn did. At the same time, Smith talks of 'continuity but not identity' between 'ethnicism' and nationalism. Nationalism is more concerned with statehood or some form of self-government than 'ethnicism', which is less clearly political. Nevertheless, 'nationalism . . . does more effectively what pre-modern ethnicists tried to do, that is, keep out foreigners and diffuse to their kinsmen the traditions and myths of their ancestors, using the modern mass education system' (p. 216).

Smith here echoes Gellner's theory of nationalism, where the latter speaks of the nation's education system and 'high culture' engendering cultural homogeneity. But Gellner saw this in functional terms: the means to economic efficiency in a developed industrial state. Smith, on the other hand, dwells on the traditional or pre-modern content to national culture, which has little to do with industrialisation. National myths, old languages, etc, are the substance of nationalism as much as modernising communications and education, and Smith's theory is better able to cope with these than Gellner's. Where Smith seems to leave questions unanswered is regarding the transition from ethnicity to nationalism, and in the strength or weakness of particular nationalisms. 'Continuity, but not identity' between ethnicity and nationalism opens up as many problems as it solves, similar to those involving the connection between human nature and nationalism, or between ethnocentrism and nationalism.

The theories discussed here are important to an understanding of nationalism, because they seek to explain how nationalism came to dominate world politics in the modern period. In comparison to the study of human nature and the study of political ideas, they stress the periodisation of history, and the particular contexts in which nationalism arose. They locate nationalism in time and place, rather than in the universals of 'ethnocentrism' and the 'idea of nationalism'. In the theories discussed in this chapter, it is apparent that developments in history are closely related to the emergence of nationalism in different parts of the world at different periods.

However, we are still some way from explaining these particular nationalisms. Once more, the 'necessary' conditions for nationalism in general are not the 'sufficient' conditions for nationalist movements to emerge and thrive. This means that we must go beyond the theories discussed so far to look for other explanations for the strengths and weaknesses of nationalist movements. We have to look at a variety of theories or explanations which focus not so much on the historical emergence of nationalism on the world scene as on contemporary nationalist political behaviour and the politics of cultural pluralism.

4
Ethnic and Social Nationalism

The idea of nationalism and the ideal of the 'nation-state' were not necessarily based on ethnicity. Rather they stressed the voluntary coming together of people in a state with a shared culture. That is how Gellner analyses the character of 'nation-states'. For him, ethnicity is not a 'given', but a construct of the state itself.

Yet in modern times, especially in the twentieth century, ethnicity has come to be more important in politics, and ethnic nationalism (or 'ethnonationalism') has been the distinguishing characteristic of one form of nationalism. In essence this is 'exclusive' nationalism, since it excludes from membership of the nation those people who do not share a common ethnicity, which usually means common descent.

A more open form of nationalism is what is here called 'social nationalism'. This is based on a shared national culture, but not on common descent. It is 'inclusive' in the sense that anyone can adopt that culture and join the nation, even if that person is not considered to be a member of the 'ethnic nation'. 'Social nationalism' can thus be distinguished from 'ethnic nationalism' on the one hand and 'official (or state) nationalism' on the other, the latter being essentially based on patriotism, with no necessary ethnic or cultural basis.

These categories are in practice not always mutually exclusive, and their meaning can be further clarified by actual examples, which show how they can be applied in the contemporary world:

Ethnic nationalism: the nationalism of ethnic groups such as the Kurds, Latvians, and Tamils, who define their nation in exclusive terms, mainly on the basis of common descent. In this type of nationalism, no one can 'become' a Kurd, Latvian, or Tamil through adopting Kurdish etc, ways.

Social nationalism: the nationalism of a nation which defines itself by social ties and culture rather than by common descent. This type of nationalism stresses the shared sense of national identity, community and culture, but outsiders can join the nation if they identify with it and adopt its social characteristics. Thus Scots, Catalans and Russians accept as members of their nations those who do not 'ethnically' belong, but who become Scots, Catalans, and Russians by joining the nation socially and culturally.

Official nationalism: the nationalism of the state, encompassing all those legally entitled to be citizens, irrespective of their ethnicity, national identity and culture. Some states are correctly called 'nation-states' in the sense that the state is exclusively composed of an eth-nic nation or a social nation. Most states, however, are multiethnic and multinational. For example, the United Kingdom consists of four nations (England, Scotland, Wales, and part of Ireland), but it is also possible to talk of a British nation and British nationalism. This 'official nation' and 'official nationalism' is based on British citizens and their patriotism. But there are also within Britain 'social nationalisms' in Scotland and Wales, with nationalist parties seeking statehood for these nations. In Northern Ireland, Irish nationalists seek the unification of Ireland, which would include all the population of the island, irrespec-tive of religion and ethnicity. There are some ethnic nationalists in Britain whose aims are 'England for the English', 'Scotland for the Scots', 'Wales for the Welsh', and 'Ireland for the Irish', but they are either on the extreme right of politics or are mainly interested in promoting cultural nationalism.

A state such as the USA is multiethnic and one social nation. While American nationalism might be considered to be no more than patriotism (official nationalism) rather than social nationalism, in fact it involves more than showing loyalty to the state. It means the adoption of American national culture, in language, education, the media, and social behaviour. Thus patriotism and cultural homogeneity go hand in hand. Britain too, while it has official nationalism, is in part an ethnic and social nation. There is much intermarriage between the ethnic groups, especially the Scots, Welsh, English and Irish, so that their separate ethnicity is now somewhat indistinct. More defined is the ethnicity of the recent immigrants from the 'New Commonwealth', who are less likely to intermarry with other ethnic groups. The 'social nation' in Britain is represented by the common British culture, espe-cially in the media, education, business and politics.

Ethnic and social nationalisms pose a threat to any state which does not have a common ethnicity or a shared identity and culture. To overcome this it must either become an ethnic nation-state, or a social nation-state, or a multinational state which guarantees ethnic or social rights to the nations within it. The last type of state will give official recognition to cultural pluralism, and its ideal constitutional form is consociational democracy (see Chapter 9). This is based on 'power-sharing' between the cultural groups (nations/ethnic groups/religious or ideological 'communities') in the state.

Why has *ethnic* nationalism come to assume such importance in contemporary politics? It may seem paradoxical that an apparently 'primordial' identity, pre-modern in origin, should be a hallmark of contemporary political behaviour. Primordial or instinctive behaviour is not bound by time, but its expression changes as the context changes. Thus what we have to understand in order to explain ethnic and social nationalism is a combination of timeless determinants of political behaviour and particular contexts.

To make this task clearer, we return to the three-fold scheme used in discussing theories of the emergence and evolution of nationalism. For we can analyse separately the political, economic and cultural aspects, and their interactions, which make up an explanation for the emergence and importance of *ethnic* and *social* nationalism, in the same way as was done for nationalism generally.

Nationalism results from changes in the character of politics, the economy and culture. However, these changes lead to ambiguous results, and it is very difficult to predict that ethnic or social nationalism, rather than some other outcome, will follow these changes. Moreover, it is clear that nationalisms in different parts of the world relate to widely differing political, economic and cultural contexts. For example, in Table 4.1, the relationship between ethnic nationalism and 'post-industrial society' and 'consumerism' is not as obviously found in Third World ethnic nationalisms, for these have a different political, economic and cultural context. Their ethnic politics is based more on primordial 'communalism' than on a sophisticated type of democratic politics arising out of an advanced economy. The new intensity of ethnic politics in the Third World can be explained only by modifying the model to take account of the different context to be found there. Even so, the *direction* of politics in the Third World is towards those features, such as democratic politics rather than Empire, and rising political consumer choice rather than monopoly. So the

Table 4.1 *Ethnic and social nationalism*

Politics	Economy	Culture
Power expectations/ capabilities	*Material interests*	*'Psychic income'*
Democracy	Uneven development and cultural division of labour	Search for identity; Increased literacy.
nation-state consociational democracy		
Nation-building (v. imperialism, internal colonialism)		Increased cultural homogeneity
Consumerism (v. centralisation) Post-industrial politics (e.g. Green parties and nationalist parties) State power v. divided nations	Decline of class divisions; Growth of status divisions 'Post-industrial society'	revival of ethnic cultures and/or 'Post-materialist values'

model above indicates a universal linkage between particular forms of politics, economy and culture. Once more, however, we are at the stage of specifying 'necessary' rather than 'sufficient' conditions, although we are all the time getting closer to the latter. When we examine specific nationalist movements in later chapters, we shall see to what extent this scheme is useful in particular cases.

Politics

In politics, the focus is on power, expressed in terms of authority and the challenge to authority. Those who achieve political power command political structures, most typically the state, but also a wide range of polities from empires to local authorities.

Those who are not in power, but who are challengers to those in power, operate in some political systems through political parties, and in others through 'movements' and terrorist organisations. In the politics of nationalism we have ruling 'National Parties', opposition nationalist parties, nationalist movements, national liberation armies, etc. Each of these relates to the nature of the state, as the focus of political power. Some nationalists seek to defend the state, others to overthrow it. The differences can be explained when one examines the ethnic nature of the state. If one ethnic group controls the state, then its nationalism is expressed as official nationalism or patriotism. Hence the ruling National Party in South Africa is essentially the party of the white Afrikaners, and the ruling United National Party in Sri Lanka is the party of the Sinhalese. But an ethnic group which does not control the state expresses its nationalism in opposition to the state. Hence, the African National Congress is opposed to the structure of the South African state, and was banned by it from 1962 to 1989. The Liberation Tigers of Tamil Eelam ('Tamil Tigers') wage war on the Sri Lankan state. Such actions as the banning of parties or movements – the Tamil United Liberation Front (TULF) in Sri Lanka, the PLO in Israel – and the imposition of direct rule from Delhi on the Punjab, undercut the local moderate parties and make it more difficult to keep ethnic nationalism on a non-violent path. Instead, extremist or terrorist organisations tend to occupy the gap left by the absence of the more moderate, representative bodies.

In a state organised along 'consociational' lines, the situation is not as polarised. Ethnic nationalist parties, and ethnic sections of state-wide parties, are not anti-state, but seek maximum power within the state. Thus the Fleming and Walloon nationalist parties in Belgium, and the Fleming and Walloon Socialist and Christian Social Parties seek the maximum power for their ethnic groups within the Belgian state on a consociational or 'power-sharing' basis.

Why has ethnic nationalism come to rival official nationalism or 'patriotism' in politics today? A purely 'political' explanation is not possible, as there are political, economic and cultural elements involved. But first, the political part can be isolated.

In politics the expectations of people have changed, and so have their capabilities. The ratio of expectations to capabilities provides the dynamic in politics generally, and nationalism is one result of this changed ratio (paradoxically, so is internationalism or supranationalism). What people have come to expect in most parts of the world is some form of democratic government: 'government by the people'. This expectation has been encouraged over a long period since the eighteenth century, but has quickened and heightened in the twentieth century. 'National self-determination' has been proclaimed as a right by politicians as widely separated in ideology as President Woodrow Wilson of the USA and Lenin and Stalin of the USSR, and more generally in the Covenant of the League of Nations and the Charter of the United Nations.

The political capabilities of people have also changed. The multi-national Empires broke up in Europe as a result of the First World War (1914–18), and in Africa and Asia after the Second World War (1939–45). War gave submerged nations their opportunity to achieve independent statehood, and those that could not be immediately 'lib-erated' waged bitter struggles for 'nationhood' (e.g., Ireland v. Britain (1918–21), and Algeria v. France (1954–62). The ability of these submerged nations to defeat powerful states marked the triumph of ethnic/social nationalism over official or state (imperial) nationalism.

The simultaneous rise of democratic expectations and the capabil-ity to achieve these through the overthrow of multinational empires was matched by the rise of nationalism within multinational states. Here, what was often involved was a nationalist reaction to 'internal colonialism' – the colonisation of subordinate ethnic groups within the state by the core ethnic group, giving rise to a 'cultural division of labour'. Internal colonialism and the cultural division of labour involve all three aspects of politics, economics and culture (see Chapter 3, under *Hechter's Theory of Internal Colonialism*).

The democratic expectation of self-government is as opposed to internal colonialism as it is to colonialism in the colonial empires. So as democracy grows in political attractiveness and is demanded for cultural communities, internal colonialism comes under attack. In this situation, many 'internal' ethnicities become mobilised politically against the state of which they are part, even when that state proclaims itself a 'nation-state'. Thus old-established states were by the mid-twentieth century threatened with break-up along with the world-wide colonial empires.

Expectations and capabilities linked both these contexts. The loss of Empire changed the expectations of many people in states that possessed such Empires, especially those groups whose position in the 'mother country' was one of a minority nation. Many Scots, who are in total just under 10% of the population of Britain, had looked to the British Empire for positions of power and wealth when these were not so easily obtained in England. When the British Empire dissolved, they found their career opportunities restricted. This meant that they had to restrict their careers more often to Britain itself, where they had to compete more sharply with the dominant English, even in Scotland. The same applied to the Basques and Catalans on the dissolution of the Spanish Empire, for they soon came into conflict with the Castilians who controlled the Madrid Government when their overseas opportunities dried up. The more that internal colonialism and cultural division of labour existed within the 'mother country', the more political conflicts between the nations resulted.

Such nationalism may not be 'separatist' in the sense of isolationist, but may seek national participation in a wider polity than the old multinational state. This of course will only satisfy nationalist feeling if the new polity is able to act along consociational rather than majoritarian lines. It may be impossible to create such a polity. This was the fate of Nkrumah's African nationalism, Pan-Africanism. This sought the establishment of a 'United States of Africa'. Pan-Africanism, like Pan-Slavism in the nineteenth century and Pan-Arabism in the 1970s, foundered on the incompatibility of nationalism with a wider formulation of political and cultural identity.

Closely related to the modern desire for democracy is consumerism. People increasingly demand the right to choose for themselves what to consume, and by analogy how to live. They have been encouraged to do this by the development of capitalism (or in socialist countries, the example of capitalism) and by the greater spending power available to most people in industrial countries. Thus consumerism usually means the demand by individuals and groups for material gain. They will decide what is the 'rational choice' for them in politics, and it may be that pursuing ethnic aims will appear rational if there is the prospect of material or some other gain (for an extended discussion of a 'rational choice' explanation of nationalist behaviour, see Tiryakian and Rogowski, 1985). In the most advanced 'post-industrial' societies, demands may go beyond economic gain to the satisfaction of 'post-materialist' values. Such values include civil rights, protection of the environment, and enhancement of such aspects of social status as ethnic identity (e.g., in language, religion, respect for the community, etc). It seems that 'post-materialist' consumerism is closely connected to ethnic nationalism, but not to official nationalism (patriotism) (see Inglehart, 1977). 'Post-materialism' will be further discussed in the section on the economy.

In political terms, this kind of consumerism seeks the availability of rights such as the right of self-government, local democracy, and cultural autonomy. Where ethnic groups are not territorially based, but consist of scattered individuals (as, for example, blacks in the US), ethnic politics involves demands for preferential treatment for members of ethnic minorities, through programmes of affirmative action, 'clientelism', and so on. As Crawford Young has pointed out (Young, 1976, pp. 23, 34), ethnic groups are mobilised in 'quintessentially modern' political situations, not on the basis of some turning back to 'primordialism'. This is because ethnic politics is appropriate to contemporary politics, especially where there is 'cultural pluralism' and a 'cultural division of labour'.

While consumerism has been encouraged by the modern democratic state, it can thus also be turned against it. Demands for decentralisation and 'home rule' for ethnic groups and social nations can be seen as consumer reactions against the modern centralised state (Sharpe, 1979, pp. 9–79). Paradoxically, when the state seeks to satisfy dissatisfied ethnic groups, as in programmes of regional economic planning to redress regional inequalities, or in the establishment of regional government agencies, it raises ethnic expectations further and demands for stronger home rule or affirmative action may follow.

In Gorbachev's USSR (i.e., since 1985), 'glasnost' (openness) and 'perestroika' (restructuring of the state and economy) have opened the floodgates to ethnic demands and capabilities to a point where many nationalities have demanded independence or autonomy within the USSR. The capability to articulate legitimately the expectations of the nationalities in the Soviet Union only became available when the Soviet state tolerated the formation of national 'Popular Fronts' and the expression of national demands at all levels of the state and Communist Party. Up till then (c. 1987), national expectations were low, and the capability to express them was circumscribed by an authoritarian regime. Thus the force of democracy and consumerism remained largely dormant until Gorbachev. Similarly, the resurgence of nationalism in Yugoslavia since the 1970s can be traced partly to political changes: the 1974 Constitution, which strengthened the powers of the national republics in the federal system; and the death of President Tito in 1980, which further weakened the central power and Yugoslav patriotism. (For further discussion of these cases, see Chapter 7.)

The examples of rising ethnic nationalism from authoritarian communist states point to the role of political vehicles such as parties,

'Popular Fronts', and semi-political cultural bodies like writers' and intellectuals' societies. For nationalism to flourish, nationalist bodies must be allowed to operate within the political system. A competitive party system with free elections will allow democratic and consumerist demands to be expressed, and these may take a nationalist form. A closed system, on the other hand, or a democratic system based on majority rule which oppresses minority nations, will lead nationalism into underground and terrorist activities. Then a struggle ensues along non-democratic lines, in which the superior forces of the state are likely to prevail, unless a civil war breaks out, in which case there is a chance that the state will be defeated, as in Algeria (1962) and Ireland (1921).

These examples show that the state is as important an actor in nationalism as the ethnic groups themselves. The state may follow a number of strategies to preserve itself in the face of a nationalist threat. It will try to 'divide and rule' a nation which threatens it. Nations are not monolithic entities, but are split into factions, ranging from extremists and terrorists to state-allied 'unionists'. Only rarely does a nationalist movement achieve majority support in its own nation for a particular course of action, and the state is thus able to manipulate the factions of the ethnic nation to its ends. These strategies may work, or they may provoke further ethnic trouble, with perhaps the disintegration of the state.

Multinational states and empires resisted nationalism at first, but those that did not see their subject nations/colonies secede through national self-determination/decolonisation, had two possibilities open to them. The first was to adopt a form of nationalism themselves ('official nationalism'), thereby seeking a new legitimacy for the state in a cultural homogeneity (ie, a new 'social nation'). Thus the Russian Empire sought to make non-Russians Russian through Russification; Britain made many Scots, Welsh and Irish 'English' through Anglicisation. This was a kind of 'nation-building' at a very late stage in the history of the state. New states in Latin America, Asia and Africa also sought to build nations out of ethnically diverse populations. It is significant that these exercises in nation-building have been only partially successful, and are particularly vulnerable to the rising demands of democracy and consumerism. The satisfaction of ethnic identity in political terms is one of these demands, and attempts at homogenisation are rejected, except where there is a clear payoff to compensate for loss of cultural identity. Internal colonialism is also attacked, and the demand is made by the subordinate nations for 'affirmative action' to redress social and economic national discrimination.

This usually leads to the adoption of an alternative accommodating strategy by multinational states (a category which of course comprises nearly all the states of the world). This strategy accepts cultural (ethnic/national) pluralism, and recognises it in the political system. Thus, the alternative to the homogeneous nation-state is the culturally plural state. This type of state varies constitutionally from a decentralised 'unitary' state such as Britain and France, to a 'confederal' or 'consociational' state such as Yugoslavia, Belgium, Switzerland, and Canada. Each multinational state has its own variation in constitutional and political terms to deal with its multinational character (for further discussion, see Chapter 9).

To sum up, the political explanation for the recent importance of ethnic nationalism is both general and particular. There is a general rise in democratic expectations and capabilities throughout the world, and this threatens multinational polities in particular; for one of the demands of consumers in a democracy is national self-government, and if the nation is perceived to be lacking in that respect, the state will come under nationalist pressure to change.

Particular developments, even events, control the politics of ethnic nationalism. A war, a change of regime, of government even, will release expectations and capabilities, or cause frustrations and resistance. Lenin, Stalin, Gorbachev, Tito, Thatcher, and Trudeau as state leaders in multinational polities have all provoked ethnic nationalism in their time. Nationalist parties and nationalist leaders for their part have also been important in organising responses from the ethnic grass-roots. Who won, and who lost, cannot be explained here (see the following chapters). There is no inevitability in the success of ethnic nationalism as compared to other political and social forces. Although ethnic politics may have become the leading force in politics in certain contexts, state, class and ideology match, and often overpower, ethnic nationalism in many cases. When such cases are studied in detail, the strengths and weaknesses of nationalism will be revealed.

Economy

If politics is about power in relation to the state, the economy concerns material interests – of individuals, firms, trade unions, 'classes', regions, nations, and so on. These, of course, impinge on political power, and it is by seeking the connection between economic and political power that we can increase our understanding of nationalism. What features of the economy are conducive to ethnic and social nationalism?

We have seen in Chapter 3 that some theorists (e.g., Gellner, and all Marxists) link the emergence of nationalism in history to a 'stage' in economic development, namely, the rise of the modern industrial or capitalist state. That is what 'caused' nationalism in their view, since the 'nation-state' is seen as functional to that particular form of economy, and nationalism occurs when the establishment of the nation-state is blocked. The continuing strength of nationalism (and racism) is also 'explained' by economics, according to these theorists. They are 'reductionists', in that they reduce nationalism to economics: for them, there is always ultimately an economic explanation for nationalism, as there is for politics and culture generally.

Such theories are of course not accepted by everyone, yet there is evidence that economic factors and material interests are indeed closely connected with nationalism. If we focus attention on the rise of ethnic and social nationalism, how do economic explanations add to our understanding?

We have seen under the heading of 'Politics' that states may be organised in such a way as to give power to one ethnic or national group. This involves economic power if such a state is seen to be based on 'internal colonialism', with a 'cultural division of labour'. In such a state, the economic opportunities of ethnic and national groups are deliberately stratified, with one group on the top and others arranged hierarchically below it.

This takes the form of 'dominant' racism or nationalism serving 'class interests' (Greenberg, 1980). It may also lead to reactive nationalism among the colonised nations, who may seek to break away from the state which oppresses them, or at least seek to redress the unfavourable balance within the state through majority rule coupled with civil rights, or through consociational democracy, federalism, devolution, regional grants, etc. Colonialism in general, of course, had a similar effect on the indigenous peoples of the colonies, who eventually sought independence from the imperial country.

A rise in nationalism, then, can be related to the economic consequences of the pursuit of a strategy of colonialism or internal colonialism, which leads to a nationalist reaction among the colonised. When such colonialism exists, a strong condition for nationalism is present, especially in an era of democracy and rising expectations, as discussed in the first section.

But it may be that no state of colonialism exists. Instead, what is likely to exist is some degree of 'uneven economic development': an economic stratification in a country which is not the result of an overt policy of the state, but the result of economic forces working 'naturally'. Thus in the world there are rich and poor states, through no merit or fault of their own, but because of the unequal distribution of the world's resources. Similarly, within a state there are rich and poor regions, with centres and peripheries in an economic sense (ie, in relation to markets, natural resources, etc).

The people of states and regions of states who feel 'relatively deprived' because of their economic situation can become politically restless in certain circumstances. They may demand changes to redress their perceived deprivation. On the other hand, they may become passive; their population may prefer emigration to rebellion, and they may become fatalists ('what is, must be'), especially where 'free market' ideas prevail.

Even in an economic system which is not one of internal colonialism, but is one of uneven development, there may be a form of 'cultural division of labour', though a less rigid one than in 'internal colonial' or 'racist' states. Rich and high status people will generally belong to the richest regions, and poor people will be concentrated in the poor regions. A 'cultural division of labour' occurs when these regions are distinguished from each other on cultural lines as well as on lines of wealth.

Where people think of themselves in ethnic or social-national terms, and inhabit a territory which is differentiated on economic grounds from other such groups, then there is a high probability that nationalism will develop, given favourable political and cultural conditions. An example of this is the strength of nationalism in Scotland and the absence of nationalism in the north of England, although both areas are poor regions in Britain, at least on some indicators. The cultural division of labour is more marked in Scotland because Scotland is a nation, while the north of England is not, although it has (non-national) cultural distinctions from other parts of England.

It is not just the poorer regions that develop nationalism, however. The rich regions may also be nationalist, if they perceive relative deprivation within the state on political and/or cultural matters. Thus, 'rich'

Catalonia and the formerly prosperous Basque lands are nationalist because of their cultural and political deprivation in Spain, especially with regard to their national language and education; so too are the Baltic nations of Estonia, Latvia, and Lithuania within the USSR, for similar (and other) reasons.

Another way of looking at this disparity between the territorial distribution of economic resources in a state and its connection with nationalism is provided by Anthony Mughan (Mughan, in Sharpe, 1979). He divides power resources into two categories: *de jure* and *de facto*. The former derive from the constitution of the state (e.g., the right to vote), while the latter concern the qualitative differences between people (e.g., their wealth, education, and so on). It is when these two types of power resource do not correspond for any one ethnic group that conflict develops. Thus a rich ethnic group which is not strong in political power will rebel, and try to change its political position. If the changes in the economy serve to reinforce an ethnic group's existing share of political power, then conflict is unlikely to occur. However, where ethnic groups gain or lose economic power while their political power stays constant or moves in the opposite direction, nationalism will develop. Mughan uses the example of Belgium to show how the rising economic power of the Flemings in a state dominated by French-speakers led to Flemish nationalism which demanded the reconstruction of the Belgian state along 'consociational' lines based on ethnicity and language. The French-speaking Walloons, for their part, also became nationalist when their primacy in *de jure* constitutional and cultural power was shown to be out-of-step with their declining economic *de facto* power.

Where a relatively poor ethnic group stays in that position as the economy develops, nationalism will not occur if the *de jure* position of that group in the state relative to the wealthy group(s) remains correspondingly weak. Perhaps the low-key nature of Scottish nationalism compared to the virulent Flemish and Walloon nationalism in Belgium in recent years can be explained by this theory. Through all the changes in the economy and politics, Scotland has remained weaker than England. Scottish nationalism took off strongly when the discoveries of oil in the North Sea off Scotland pointed to a relative shift in economic wealth in Britain towards Scotland. This led to demands for a reconstruction of the constitution of the British state through devolution or federalism, and for its dissolution through Scottish independence. The relative decline in the Scottish economy after 1979 reinforced the correspondence between *de facto* and *de jure* power, and Scottish nationalism was only able to revive when the balance was again upset after 1987. Scotland's constitutional position seemed to deteriorate when the Conservative Government imposed unpopular policies on Scotland with only 10 out of 72 MPs in Scotland. Scotland seemed to be effectively disfranchised since its votes counted for nothing in the formation of British Governments or their policies for Scotland. At the same time, the Scottish economy improved, and something of a cultural renaissance accelerated. So a disjunction between economic, political and cultural power took place, which contributed to a rise in nationalism. This interpretation corresponds with Stein Rokkan's analysis of regionalism as resulting from an 'incongruity between cultural, economic and political roles' (Rokkan and Urwin, 1983, p. 192).

When the focus turns to ethnic and national groups whose base is not territorial but within the labour force of a multicultural society, a similar economic explanation for nationalism, ethnic politics and racism is given by some theorists. In this context, the cultural division of labour operates within the economy to stratify individuals according to their ethnic origin: an ethnic-class system. Thus, black migrant workers tend to be at the bottom of the class hierarchy, for reasons related to the 'supply and demand' of their labour, but also because of their ethnicity and their class position in the country they came from (Indians and Pakistanis have different class origins from Afro-Americans). They are doubly discriminated against: economically as a 'lower class' in the labour force *and* culturally because they are ethnically different from the higher classes of the labour force (Miles, 1982; Enloe, 1973; Greenberg, 1980). This analysis has particular reference to 'ethnic politics' and racism in cities, where ethnic groups compete for scarce resources in a modern economy. They compete in the economy as ethnic groups rather than as individuals to the extent that the state and the economy discriminates between them on ethnic lines (e.g., according to a cultural division of labour). This discrimination may be negative (against their interests) or positive (in their favour). The former is a denial of opportunities on account of ethnic identity, ranging from the informal to the state-sponsored (e.g., apartheid), while the latter is typified by programmes of 'affirmative action' to favour disadvantaged ethnic groups (usually blacks) in the United States. In both contexts ethnic groups assert their identity for economic reasons; there seems to be a disadvantage in so doing in the former case, and an advantage in the latter. The alternative of assimilation is effectively blocked under an Apartheid system based on skin colour, and so ethnic groups continue to assert their ethnicity. And there are political disadvantages present in a system of affirmative action, for not only will some members of the favoured groups prefer to seek assimilation or to compete on the same terms as members of other groups, but the groups not covered by affirmative action programmes may rebel against them as a denial of political equality.

These examples show that material, economic interests are at stake in ethnic politics, with groups and individuals seeking an advantage, usually by playing up their ethnicity to secure scarce resources. At the same time, there is an alternative strategy of assimilation, favoured in certain circumstances.

The relationship between the economy and nationalism is not static but dynamic. Indeed, as we have seen, it is the **changes** in political, economic and cultural relationships which give rise to nationalism. The technological changes which have occurred in the late twentieth century have altered the types of employment and the 'classes' in the labour force in 'advanced industrial countries' (and to a lesser extent in other countries as well). The division of interest between the 'working class' and the 'middle class', which was reflected in 'class politics' is no longer so obvious, as people see their interests increasingly in terms other than 'class'. A great deal of political science is devoted to charting this development in political behaviour in western Europe and in North America. What is apparent is that while people still vote predominantly according to their assessment of their material interests seen in economic terms, they no longer do so in terms of class interests, if class is seen in dichotomous terms ('working class'/'middle class'). Thus in Britain, the Labour Party now gets under half the 'working class vote', and the Conservatives cannot rely entirely on the 'middle class vote'. 'Non-class parties' such as centre parties, Green parties, and Nationalist parties have gained many votes at the expense of the 'class parties' in many countries. This change in voting reflects changes in the economy, and in the nature of material interests. As regards nationalist politics, it is the decline of class politics which opens up an increased potential for nationalist political behaviour, including nationalist voting.

Why should nationalism take the place of 'class politics', at least up to a point? In part the answer lies in the discussion above. Material economic interests *are* served by nationalism in certain circumstances, or can be seen to be served by it. This is especially true where a simple 'class division' of interests is not present because of a cultural division of labour. But there is a more general reason for nationalism to eclipse class politics in many countries today, and that is the increasing importance in 'post-industrial societies' of 'quality of life' issues as compared to 'materialist' or class issues. As Ronald Inglehart puts it:

> The values of Western publics have been shifting from an overwhelming emphasis on material well-being and physical security towards greater emphasis on the quality of life. (Inglehart, 1977, p. 3)

Non-materialist politics are, curiously enough, present in countries which are either 'pre-industrial' or 'post-industrial'. In both cases, nationalism occurs strongly today, although pre-industrial societies are not considered by commentators such as Gellner to display nationalism. Today, countries in the Third World which have not yet industrialised nevertheless display nationalism or ethnic divisions rather than class divisions because class has not yet developed widely as an alternative cleavage.

Post-industrial societies, on the other hand, have gone through the industrialising phase, and are now apparently entering a 'post-industrial' phase where 'post-materialist values' compete with material interests. These values tend to focus on such things as the quality of the environment and on civil rights and cultural matters. Economic or class interests are not strongly articulated because there is a high degree of economic and physical security in these societies.

In place of class divisions come status divisions. Clearly, this is one possible explanation for nationalism arising in advanced 'post-industrial societies', for it is only when class divisions fade that status divisions such as identity, language, culture and nationality can assume major importance. Thus nationalism is likely to occur when the class cleavages of industrial society are weak, and this can be both before and after the main period of industrialisation.

Culture

Culture differs from economy as 'psychic income' differs from financial income or material interests. 'Psychic income' refers to those things which satisfy the mental and spiritual needs of human beings; material interests are those things which are readily quantifiable in cash terms, such as incomes and jobs. Of course, it is impossible to draw the line in any precise manner: money can buy culture, and jobs can be obtained in education and the arts.

Culture also reintroduces the discussion of 'status' and 'class'. Culture is more linked to status, while material interests form the basis of class. Essentially, class refers to an economic situation, while status involves identity, prestige, inner satisfaction, etc.

Nationality and culture are almost synonymous. This is because both include a sense of social identity, a language, education, religion, the arts, science and so on. While some culture may be cosmopolitan, many of its attributes are national. For nationalism, the place of culture is vital. Without a national culture there would be little left of nationhood, certainly of ethnic and social nationhood (state or official nationalism, on the other hand, may be multicultural). Thus in the formula 'Politics + Economy + Culture = Nationalism', there is a special weight for culture.

What changes in culture have been conducive to a rise in ethnic and social nationalism? And what changes have been contrary to such nationalism – that is, conducive to official (state) nationalism or cosmopolitanism? Is the balance today favourable to nationalism, or against it?

The search for identity in the conditions of the modern world has led to increased ethnic and social nationalism in some cases, and increased official nationalism and cosmopolitanism in others. Why this ambiguity? In part it is the result of the different characteristics of economic systems which have developed. Gellner pointed to the imperatives of the industrial state in the emergence of nationalism: homogeneous national cultures within one state go hand-in-hand with industrial economies, according to him, and are indeed necessary to them. Thus a social and cultural identity flows from the needs of the economy, and is promoted by the state.

As we have seen in the previous discussion of Gellner, there is ambiguity here. If Gellner is right in his general approach, then as the economy internationalises, the national characteristics fade into cosmopolitan ones, and with them fade the national cultures. To some extent that has happened, and nationalism has weakened at the state level. However, it is difficult to explain sub-state ethnic and social nationalism from Gellner's theory. His theory postulates that as the state economy predominates over local and regional economies, so too state identity, state culture, and official nationalism will predominate over ethnic and social identity, culture and nationalism. Yet what we are faced with is the opposite: the rise of ethnic and social nationalism in opposition to state nationalism.

Of course, this may be a temporary reaction to an inevitable centralising process, and ethnic and social nationalism may face ultimate defeat by state nationalism, or cosmopolitanism. Yet when we examine the strength of culture in nationalism, we find that it seems as powerful as politics and economy, and that in the conditions of sudden change in the modern world people turn to their ethnic and (nearest) social culture as a defence against deprivation in politics and material interests. This is not a throw-back to ancient ways, but a very up-to-date way of defending personal and group interests. It is also dependent on modern cultural developments which, contrary to Gellner's theory, do not contribute to state homogeneity, or state nationalism. As Dogan and Pelassy put it in *How to Compare Nations*:

> The development of media, transportation, school enrollment, or urbanization paradoxically does not necessarily favor a homogenization of society. Indeed, these very elements that objectively unify styles of living at the same time provide minorities with the means of subjectively recognizing themselves as conscious entities. (Dogan and Pelassy, 1984, p. 52)

So what we should look for in explaining how cultural developments have contributed to the rise of ethnic and social nationalism, in opposition to state nationalism or cosmopolitanism, is the presence and strength of a substate educational system, with its associated intelligentsia, a substate media system, and a set of cultural organisations which support the local language, arts, historical studies, etc, as a distinct culture of the ethnic or social nation.

These things have of course been well studied in the *history* of nationalism, but there are *contemporary* developments which have led to renewed cultural nationalism. First, there has been a big increase in literacy, through the spread of education to all people. The opportunities to promote national culture have steadily increased with the spread of mass publications, and these are often accessible to nationalists, unless the state exercises censorship and monopolises printing (as in most communist states). There has also been an immense spread of the broadcast media, notably television. If there is a national language which has been suppressed or discouraged by the state, linguistic questions are likely to be a rallying point for ethnic and social nationalism, and will get exposure in the press and broadcast media. A separate Welsh language TV channel was granted in 1982, after a hunger-strike by the Welsh Nationalist President, Gwynfor Evans.

All this has led to competing messages reaching people, and competing cultures arriving right inside the home, where before perhaps only one culture was dominant. One of these cultures is that of the ethnic and social nation, no longer 'home-bred' but systematically refined by national cultural leaders, many of them 'cultural nationalists'. They articulate to the widest possible audience the claims of the nation to cultural autonomy and survival. This gives confidence to those disposed towards nationalism, since they become aware of the nation's cultural identity as something valuable and respectable, and not something to be ashamed of in the face of the culture of the state or cosmopolitan culture. They are able to share their national identity with opinion leaders, and to learn from them what their national culture is, and how it should be defended.

Most minority nations feel that their culture is under attack from the state, which usually identifies with the majority nation or with a synthetic state culture. This leads to a sense of cultural deprivation among many in the minority nations. 'Relative deprivation' is closely linked to nationalism, and can take the form of political, economic, or cultural deprivation. Cultural deprivation in the context of nationalism is experienced when discrimination or insult takes place on account of a person's national identity, language (including accent), religion, habits, tastes, and so on.

This occurs most frequently, of course, when face-to-face contact takes place between dominant and dominated nationals, but it is also experienced collectively, and at a distance, as when linguistic or educational usages are imposed officially on all citizens by the state. These emanate from the capital city, through laws or regulations, but they are often left to fellow nationals to enforce. All this leads to a sense of cultural deprivation, and this kind of deprivation is at least as important in explaining nationalist behaviour as its more celebrated counterpart, relative economic deprivation. Examples of cultural deprivation in motivating nationalism abound throughout the world, and two examples from Scotland illustrate it. Billy Wolfe, Chairman of the SNP from 1969 to 1979, writes in his autobiography, *Scotland Lives* (Wolfe, 1973, p. 8), that in the British Army

> I was constantly exposed to the English middle-class assertion that the anglicised (they called it 'the civilised') Scot was the best kind of person in the world (a world in which only English was spoken).

Another (current) leading figure in the SNP, Jim Sillars, recalls that when he served in the British Navy, 'I could understand them but they either could not or refused to understand me' (Sillars, 1986, p. 11). In Portsmouth (naval base) people 'delighted in taking the mickey by refusing to understand a single word I said'. Years later, his first speech in the House of Commons after his election in 1988 was greeted with taunts from English Tory MPs, 'Speak English!', which no doubt strengthened his cultural nationalism.

These are nationalists who point to personal cultural deprivation to explain their nationalism. Collective cultural deprivation also leads to nationalism, and is present when cultural organisations and educational bodies fight for the national culture against assimilation with other cultures and education systems. Thus the Educational Institute of Scotland, the largest teachers' union in Scotland, ran a press advertising campaign in 1988 against the 'Anglicisation' of Scottish education through the introduction of reforms patterned on English practice. Cultural deprivation also motivates nationalism in the Soviet Republics, Belgium (especially Flanders), Quebec, Wales, Corsica, Catalonia, the Basque lands, and many other nations. Any nation whose identity is based on language, religion, education or the Arts, and which is faced with threats to its culture, is likely to react with nationalism.

Is cultural nationalism on the increase, or is it merely a losing battle against assimilation and cosmopolitanism? As we have seen, the technological opportunities for cultural nationalism are increasing, in publications and broadcasting. These can assert national cultures, and if there is a 'cultural division of labour', then material interests will reinforce cultural ones: class and status will be combined. Moreover, the 'search for identity' and the pursuit of 'psychic income' are features of 'post-materialist society'.

Culture matters more as class and materialism decline in significance as the focus of political conflict. This may be because class interests are now less salient since they have been transformed into sectional interests. Nationalism cuts across class and sectional interests, and it can only succeed when classes and sections lose their ability to command supreme loyalty. In cultural nationalism people unite to pursue something different from personal, sectional or class interest – their status as members of the nation.

The apparent decline of class conflict in many modern societies gives nationalism its opportunity, and the rise of cultural nationalism shows that cultural conflicts are as important as economic ones. While much is ambiguous about the changing nature of politics, economy and culture and how such change contributes to the rise of ethnic and social nationalism, the weights in the equation have shifted from those which favoured official state nationalism and cosmopolitanism to those which emphasise ethnic and social nationalism. But such preconditions for nationalist behaviour are only made into strong political nationalism by the activities of nationalist movements and parties, to which we now turn.

5

Nationalist Movements and Ethnic Politics

In this chapter, the focus is on the forms of nationalist movements and ethnic politics, and the nature of their support. The aim is to give a historical and geographic perspective to the study of nationalism. There is also a discussion of the nature of nationalist political behaviour, the social characteristics of nationalists, and the circumstances in which nationalist movements and ethnic politics succeed or fail. In the next three chapters, case studies are given of nationalist movements and ethnic politics in different parts of the world today.

Forms of Nationalism and Ethnic Politics

Pre-Nationalism and Ethnic Politics

For most writers on nationalism, nationalism is a modern political ideology which can be found only from the late eighteenth century. 'National consciousness', however, is traced back to ancient times (Kohn, 1944), and nations are held to have 'ethnic origins' (Smith, 1986).

It seems that many of these distinctions are rather artificial. There are clear examples of pre-modern nationalism in Scotland, England, France, and among the Jews, although there was no clear political role for 'the people' until the ideology of democracy took root after the French Revolution. Thus 'national self-determination' and 'popular sovereignty' were principles which had to await the era of representative government and democracy.

It is also the case that many 'nationally conscious' nations did not seek statehood until modern times. For example, it was the Zionist ideology of the late nineteenth century which made many Jews support

72

the aim of a 'national home' in Palestine. But Jews had always been highly nationalist (or at least ethnically exclusive) during the period of the 'diaspora' (dispersal throughout the world).

'Official nationalism' or nation-building is found in the pre-modern period in western Europe, with states such as England, France, Spain and Portugal consolidating their hold over the people with appeals to patriotism, and with the construction of national languages, literature, educational institutions, and so on. Here, the 'state' preceded the 'nation', and nationalism meant nation-building.

In most other parts of the world nations remained largely at the ethnic and social level. Nationalism was not 'official', since states did not usually seek to be national in character. Rather, they were either multinational or multiethnic empires, kingdoms, etc, or, in what is called the 'Third World' today, 'tribal' or 'communal' polities. In these states, 'imperialism' and 'ethnic politics', rather than nationalism, predominated.

It is possible to view some contemporary Third World politics as 'pre-nationalist', since in these tribalism and multiethnic states are to be found. However, the fact is that nationalism is a world-wide ideology today, and it influences the Third World as much as the 'First' and 'Second' Worlds. So it is impossible to isolate politics in the Third World from the effects of the nationalist ideals of self-determination and cultural homogeneity. Thus 'pre-nationalist' politics properly belongs to a *period* before the spread of nationalist ideology, rather than to *places* in the world today.

Classical European Nationalism

As we have seen in Chapter 2, the ideology of nationalism seems to have originated in Europe. It then spread throughout the world in the nineteenth century. But this nationalism, even within Europe, was divided into a 'western' and an 'eastern' form. The 'western' nationalism was ethnically 'inclusive' in that it was based on a 'social nation' which could encompass more than one ethnic group. It was essentially about the cultural homogeneity of the state, and the common citizenship of those sharing that culture. 'Eastern' European national-ism, on the other hand, was ethnically 'exclusive' and was focused on the nation as a community of common descent, language, and religion. In 'western European nationalism', the existing citizens of a territory were acceptable as members of the nation, and could form a 'nation-state'. In 'eastern European nationalism', only those with the correct ethnic credentials had the right to live in a territory and be the citizens of the nation-state.

The forms taken by nationalist movements in Europe set the pattern for nationalisms throughout the world. The inclusive nationalisms were more liberal and democratic, and did not engage in genocide, transfers of population, etc. The exclusive nationalisms were intolerant and often led to authoritarianism. Examples of the former are Irish, Scottish, Catalan and Norwegian nationalisms, and of the latter, Bulgarian, Turkish, Tamil and Sikh nationalisms.

Of course, these categories are not rigid. In Northern Ireland, exclusive nationalism prevails, and 'Greater Serbian' nationalism is more inclusive. In the centre of Europe, German nationalism is a combination of ethnic nationalism, based on language and the concept of 'Volk' (common descent), and social or official nationalism based on citizenship of the German state, whatever form that takes (otherwise known as 'traditional' nationalism based on the 'lesser' German nation or *kleindeutsch*).

During the nineteenth century various strategies of nationalist movements became apparent:

Unification Movements

The unification of the German nation and of the Italian nation in the late nineteenth century was accomplished through war and conquest of existing states. Usually a core state (the Kingdom of Prussia in Germany and the Kingdom of Sardinia in Italy) expanded its power over other states which constituted the 'nation', and either annexed them or left them virtually powerless (as Bavaria in Germany or Venetia in Italy). This type of nationalism is also called 'Risorgimento' (rebirth) nationalism, after the Italian nationalist movement, and it combined the aim of national unification with liberal ideals of democracy and freedom from oppression (for a useful account of the forms of nationalism, see Alter, 1989, whose scheme is partly followed here).

National Secession Movements

In most cases, nationalism led to the break-up of existing states, not their joining together in one large 'nation-state'. So nationalist movements in Ireland, Greece, Poland, Serbia, and Norway, for example, achieved independence for their nations by breaking away from Britain, the Ottoman Empire, the Russian Empire, the Austrian Empire, and Sweden, respectively. Today, national secession movements are still active in Europe: in Scotland, Wales, the Basque country, Corsica, Slovenia, Croatia, Lithuania, Latvia and Estonia, and so on. Of course, these vary greatly in the intensity of their nationalism and in the degree of popular support given to them.

Reform Nationalism

This kind of nationalism occurred in Japan in the mid-nineteenth century, and in Turkey in the early twentieth century. It was also seen in part in China, Egypt and Persia (Iran) after 1921. As with 'risorgimento' nationalism the aim was national 'rebirth', but it was confined to an existing state, and the nationalists were the traditional ruling class, not a new anti-establishment group. The strategies were economic modernisation, the defence of national identity, and independence from foreign control. Thus the Japanese, Turks, Chinese, Egyptians and Persians fought off European imperialists and established modern nation-states. Reform nationalism took different forms: in Japan it was focused on the Emperor; in Turkey on the Young Turks and secularisation; in Persia on the Shah. All were 'nationalists' in their antipathy to foreigners and their sponsorship of a national language and culture.

Integral Nationalism

Integral nationalism differs from 'risorgimento' nationalism in its belief that one's nation is superior to all others, and may even be the result of biological natural selection. 'Risorgimento' nationalism, on the other hand, is liberal in its attitude towards other nationalisms, believing them to be equal in status, even if their claims may be mutually incompatible (e.g., *irredentism* is a form of nationalism which lays claim to the territory of another state).

Integral nationalism is an absolutist ideology (the absolute loyalty to the nation is demanded), and in politics is clearly linked to totalitarian, Fascist, and Nazi forms of government. Its main examples are Mussolini's Italy, Hitler's Germany, Franco's Spain, and Action Française in late nineteenth century France.

Colonial Nationalism

In the European colonial empires (especially the British, Spanish, Portuguese, Dutch, and French), a nationalism developed among the European settlers, which led to the independence of the colonies from the mother country. The Americans showed the way in 1776, followed by the Spanish and Portuguese in Latin America in the early nineteenth century. By the late nineteenth century, Canadians, Australians, South Africans (both British and Afrikaner), and New Zealanders had displayed their nationalism in new nation-states, even if this was often tinged with a 'dual identity' with the mother country.

The most recent examples of colonial 'settler' nationalisms are the French Algerian nationalists of the 1950s and early 1960s and the British Rhodesian settlers, with their 'unilateral declaration of independence' in 1965. These settlers were seeking secession in order to maintain their own internal (racist) hegemony at a time when the Mother country wanted to liberalise the situation. Both these 'colonial' nationalisms failed, when the metropolitan power successfully asserted its authority (unlike the earlier examples).

The settlement of Israel by Zionist Jews in the twentieth century provides an interesting hybrid between colonial nationalism and integral or exclusive nationalism. The 'colonisation' of Palestine was based on an ancient ethnic claim to its homeland by the Jews. The 'native' Palestinians are inclined to view the Israelis as 'settlers', which makes Palestinian nationalism more akin to anti-colonialism, and Zionism similar to 'risorgimento' nationalism.

Anti-Colonial Nationalism

Anti-colonialism is the last form of nationalism dealt with here. The emergence of indigenous 'national liberation' and anti-colonial movements in the British Empire corresponded with the spread of nationalist ideology from Europe. Thus, unification and risorgimento nationalisms were to be found in the colonies of Africa and Asia. So too was 'Pan-Africanism' and the complex mix of religion and nationalism in Asia.

Given the existing colonial state structure at independence, the nationalists of the new 'nation-states' had to preserve boundaries which reflected the boundaries of colonial power rather than cultural or national divisions. Thus 'nation-building', irredentisms, and secessions were permanently on the agenda of nearly all these new states. Now nationalism did not usually mean anti-colonialism, except in the form of hostility to 'dependency' on the former colonial powers (re-categorised as 'neo-colonialism'). Instead it meant interethnic disputes, communalism, and sometimes genocide. In this situation, the development of political parties along ethnic lines, and of ethnic 'liberation armies' subverted the stability of the states which had succeeded the colonies. Only ethnic accommodation and 'consociational democracy' seemed to offer a way out of this predicament.

Consociationalism and Multiethnic Politics

The twentieth century has seen an attempt to make democracy compatible with a 'culturally plural' society. This represents an alternative to the classic aim of nationalism, which was to form a 'nation-state' out of one homogeneous nation or ethnic group.

The Swiss were the first (from the Middle Ages) to show the way to combine several linguistic and religious peoples in one highly decentralised system of government. Later, in the 1970s, the Belgians 'federalised' their state to give equality to the Flemings and Walloons. From the 1940s, wherever one state contained several nations or ethnic groups, and sought to establish democratic government on the basis not of majority rule but through consensus between minorities, then some form of consociationalism was adopted. Such attempts were made in Lebanon, Yugoslavia, Nigeria, Malaysia, Sri Lanka, India, Northern Ireland and South Africa. The success rate has not been high, as many of these experiments collapsed, or were not properly attempted in the first place. However, each of these multicultural states is still trying to produce another version of consociationalism, for that 'model' of government remains the main democratic alternative to the nation-state in conditions of territorially-based multiculturalism (for an extended discussion, see Chapter 9).

Within a nation-state, there may be ethnic minorities whose claims cannot be met by territorial consociationalism. These are groups who do not possess a territory they can call their 'home'. They are usually recent immigrants, marked off from the rest of the population by their ethnicity and social class. A multicultural or multiethnic society of this kind exists in most western states, including the United States, Canada, Britain, France and Germany. 'Ethnic politics' has developed in these countries, and it differs from nationalism in that the ethnic groups accept the constitutional structure of the state. They seek to use the constitution to their advantage, through their votes (occasionally but not usually forming ethnic parties), pressure group activity, and promoting legal changes to outlaw discrimination, provide for 'affirmative action', minority language/religious/educational rights, and so on. The more pronounced these demands are, and the bigger the minority groups, the more the state will tend towards consociationalism on the basis of non-territorial 'individual' and 'group' rights. The working-out of a political form to take account of this type of multicultural society is still in its infancy.

The Social Origins of Nationalists

Who is likely to be a nationalist, or to support a nationalist movement? In the previous discussion, we have seen that nationalism is found in many different contexts, both in history and across the world. It can be divided into 'official nationalism', 'social nationalism', and 'ethnic nationalism'. Thus it can be espoused by the governments of states, and by those who seek to overthrow these governments. While the theories discussed in earlier chapters have examined the general political, economic and cultural conditions in which nationalism emerged and evolved, they have not clearly pinpointed the nature of nationalist support nor the reasons for the political successes and failures of nationalist movements. Without nationalist activists, organised in nationalist parties and political organisations, nationalism would be largely ineffective politically.

'Nationalists' should not be defined as one homogeneous group. Even if we focus on nationalist parties alone, we can distinguish between nationalist leaders, activists, party members, and those who merely vote nationalist in elections. All of these differ in their social characteristics and political motivation. Moreover, what can be called nationalist political behaviour is found beyond the confines of nationalist parties and organisations. It is also to be seen in other parties, in trade unions, and in cultural bodies. In particular, European socialist and Green Parties now support devolution to regions and nations, and sometimes total national independence (e.g., the Scottish Green Party). So we must extend our analysis to these. Finally, the interaction of nationalists with those who do not display social or ethnic nationalist behaviour (and who may be actively anti-nationalist in that sense, though they may be 'official nationalists') to a large extent determines the characteristics of anti-state nationalists and whether their political actions will succeed or not.

All this seems to imply that few, if any, generalisations can be made about nationalists and their political behaviour. But that is not really the case. There is often common ground between the many studies of nationalist movements, even if the contexts of these are very different. This gives some hope that a general theory of nationalist political behaviour is possible.

One study which generalises about the social origins of nationalists across nations is by the Czech historian Miroslav Hroch (Hroch, 1985). Hroch's work has been widely used by students of nationalist movements, and he shows that nationalist movements in nineteenth century Europe drew support from different social groups at different phases of their development. In the first phase, the cultural one, some members of the middle and upper classes developed an interest in national history, language and culture, and supported organisations devoted to promoting these. No clear political aims were voiced at this stage. The second phase, however, involved people of a similar social type in voicing political demands for home rule, usually in pressure groups rather than in nationalist parties. This mobilised support for nationalist demands in the people as a whole. The third and last phase saw the establishment of nationalist movements as mass movements, with nationalist parties and political organisations. The most extreme nationalists were now satisfied with nothing less than total political independence for their nation, and their support was broadened to include the mass of the people. These phases of nationalism are linked by Hroch to the phases of economic and cultural change in the countries concerned.

Hroch's categorisation of the phases of nationalist movements is useful, and has been applied to other cases. Hroch was examining the nationalist movements of the 'smaller European nations' in the nineteenth century, and it is not clear that his analysis is as applicable to contemporary politics, or to non-European contexts. It can be said that while his conclusions are still relevant, the 'phases' of nationalist activity today are less clearly separated. In contemporary nationalist movements, these phases have been largely compressed into one. All nationalist movements today are mass movements, at least in aim, and the division between 'cultural', 'political' and 'economic' nationalism is not a matter of development over time, but a division among nationalists. To that extent it remains true that cultural, political and economic nationalists can be distinguished socially from each other.

In contemporary nationalist movements, cultural nationalists are usually drawn from the education world or the creative arts, especially writing and broadcasting. Here we can see that a 'vested interest' in nationalism is involved, for the livelihood of such people is bound up with the nation's identity. Teaching a national language, writing it, and broadcasting it, brings such people economic gains and a reason to favour nationalist political behaviour, though not always to the point of supporting a nationalist party. Usually nations possess educational and cultural institutions, even if they do not have statehood or autonomy. Workers in such institutions are the backbone of nationalist movements. They are not recognisable as being economically deprived but may be considered part of a 'segmental cultural division of labour' in Hechter's terms (Hechter in Tiryakian and Rogowski, 1985, p. 22). This means that their occupations are identified with the nation, and that they defend their economic interests in a way which can be described as nationalist political behaviour.

Nationalists are also drawn from the ranks of the economically deprived, and their poor economic position may lead to nationalism even if their occupations are not 'national' in any cultural sense. For example, industrial workers threatened with unemployment may be nationalist if it seems to them that their nation has been discriminated against by the state. Once more, the 'cultural division of labour' is involved, and even 'internal colonialism', if members of a nation perceive themselves to be exploited by the dominant nation. It might be predicted from the theory of internal colonialism that those who suffer most economically and socially from such colonialism would be the most nationalist. But such people may perceive their deprivation in class rather than national terms, and may prefer to support a socialist party rather than a nationalist one. Nationalist parties find it difficult to get working class support where socialist parties offer remedies for their economic complaints, but the credibility of such remedies varies according to the political context. In general, nationalists tend to come from intermediate social positions, rather than from the ranks of the poor or the rich, who are more attracted to 'class parties'.

Paradoxically, the 'cultural division of labour' leads to nationalism or racism among those who assert their economic superiority over other nations or races within the state. In racist societies, dominant classes sustain their power and economic advantages through racist economic and social practices and a racist state structure (Greenberg, 1980).

But even in non-racist states, dominant economic-cultural groups may resent having to subsidise the poorer nations in the state, and may seek political independence for their nation so that they can keep its superior resources to themselves. Examples of these 'wealthy' nationalists are to be found among the Flemings in Belgium, the Baltic nations in the USSR, the Catalans and Basques in Spain, and those Scots who proclaimed in the 1970s and 1980s that the new-found wealth off Scotland in North Sea oil made them 'Rich Scots' compared to 'Poor Britons'.

It must always be remembered, however, that only a proportion of any nation exhibits strong nationalist behaviour. What that proportion is depends on the particular circumstances of the situation. In most cases, the divisions among nations are as important as their features of unity, and this is particularly true of elite groups in the nation. There are three main types of elite: the **political** elite, encompassing established politicians, civil servants and the military; the **cultural** elite, especially teachers, writers and clergy; and the **economic** elite, comprising businessmen and trade union leaders. Each of these reacts differently towards nationalism and towards the central state. As we have seen, where there is a strong national culture, the cultural elite is likely to be nationalist. The economic elite is likely to be the least nationalist, especially if its links with wider markets and firms are strong. The position of the political elite is crucial, and it is only when it fragments that nationalism is able to make progress. Even so, there is always a segment of that elite which remains loyal to the state, or which exploits the state from within on behalf of the nation, without going over to the nationalist side. The balance here is a shifting one, and the centre may be so unsympathetic to nationalist demands that some centrist 'go-betweens' find their role unviable, and turn towards nationalism. This was for example the case in Ireland after 1916, when nearly all M. P.s and local officials in the South of Ireland supported the break from Britain. It has also happened recently in the Basque country, Catalonia, and the Baltic nations of the USSR. In these cases the hostile reaction of the state was as important to nationalist behaviour as the demands of the nation itself.

While these observations about the links between occupation and nationalist behaviour provide a general context for the study of nationalism, it is by no means clear that nationalists are related in any systematic way to the social structure, although there are tendencies towards regularities. In Scotland, most nationalist activists are

employed in Scottish cultural, educational and local government institutions; in small businesses; or are self-employed. They are rarely
managers or employees in large firms. Perhaps this is because the
large firms, and their associated trade unions, are less identified with
the nation than with the state and the international economy, and
they may fear that nationalism will threaten their prosperity by set-
ting up trade barriers and extra taxation. However, it is not possible
to predict how many people in a given social category will behave
in a nationalist manner, until other political factors are taken into
account.

These can only be discovered in the history of each nation. For
example, nationalists in different parts of Spain differ from each other
in social characteristics, according to the histories and economies of
their nations, and because of the policies of the Spanish state towards
them. Nationalists in Catalonia are distinctly more middle class and
wealthy than many nationalists in the Basque country. In the latter
nation, industrialists have traditionally supported the Spanish state as
an internal free market and external protection for their trade. In the
late nineteenth century they achieved the abolition of the customs
barrier between the Basque country and the rest of Spain, and with
it most of Basque autonomy. The decline of the Spanish Empire in the
twentieth century and the suppression of Basque culture by General
Franco (in power, 1939–75) converted many Basque businessmen
to the nationalist cause. Today, Basques are divided politically along
class and ethnic lines. Immigrant and urban workers tend to support
the Socialists, the middle class the moderate nationalists (PNV), and
the urban unemployed and small farmers the separatist Herri Batasuna
party (HB) and its associated paramilitary body ETA (Keating, 1988,
pp. 214–7; Sullivan, 1988). The more prosperous Catalans are not
as drawn to extreme nationalism, and there is no equal counterpart to
ETA and HB in Catalonia (Keating, 1988, p. 225).

This is related to the more repressive policies of the Spanish state
towards the Basques than towards the Catalans. Basque nationalists
were able to gather support from many people before 1975 as they
strongly opposed the unpopular Franco regime. The threat of Basque
separatism provoked an attempted military coup in Madrid in 1981
which had the aim of reversing the decentralising Constitution of 1978.
This shows how nationalism within a state can lead to an extreme
centrist reaction, even though the ruling nationalist parties in the Basque
lands and Catalonia are autonomists rather than separatists.

Religious leaders are prominent in nationalist movements in some cases. This may be because religion is a strong national identifier, as in Poland and Armenia, or because church leaders are relatively free to express political dissent in authoritarian regimes (e.g., South Africa). Writers and scholars are also notable nationalists. In 1989, the writer Vaclav Havel became President of Czechoslovakia, and the musicologist Vytautas Landsbergis the President of Lithuania.

The presence of immigrant workers complicates the pattern of political behaviour. On the one hand, they often provoke nationalism among the indigenous workers. On the other hand, these immigrant workers swell the vote for state-wide class parties (usually socialist). Thus in Catalonia and the Basque country, the Spanish Socialist Party gets much support from the large number of workers who have moved there from other parts of Spain. Similarly, in the Baltic nations of Estonia, Latvia and Lithuania, the Russian immigrants oppose Baltic nationalism and are largely loyal to the USSR and the Communist Party of the Soviet Union. But socialist and other governing parties in western Europe, and now even some in the CPSU, have responded to nationalist demands by granting moderate home rule forms of government, thereby seeking to contain nationalism through concessions. This can be considered a form of nationalist behaviour by non-nationalists, though cynics might say it is just a devious way to defeat the nationalists without really granting any power to their nations. This strategy, however, tends to backfire when nationalist demands escalate as frustration is felt.

Nationalist Political Behaviour

The extent of nationalist political behaviour is difficult to determine, for it is found not just in nationalist parties and organisations but in other parties and organisations as well. However, the nationalism of these other bodies is usually a reaction to the demands and successes of the self-confessed nationalists, and it is best to concentrate on these in the first place.

At one end of the spectrum, nationalists seem to encompass all those expressing national identity, ethnocentrism, and some kind of economic and social interest in the nation. It is all too easy when discussing nationalism to assume that all 'Scots' or 'Catalans' or 'Tamils' share a common nationalist political behaviour, especially when nationalist parties are doing well in elections, or when extreme nationalist organisations are hitting the headlines in campaigns of violence. Commentators in the newspapers and in broadcasting copy the nationalists themselves when they 'reify' the nation by attributing to it a single will, which is in reality not present. The nation is always divided into the wills of particular individuals and groups, and its political behaviour is similarly divided. In the nation there are nationalists and anti-nationalists, and divisions among the nationalists themselves, with separatists and autonomists often forming their own parties. These divisions are a source of weakness for nationalism, despite its great strength in politics throughout the world. For they can allow the anti-nationalists or official nationalists to 'divide and rule' a nation in many cases. If a nation were truly united, its will might be irresistible. But there is never 100 per cent nationalist behaviour in any nation with one aim. The opposing 'unionists' use official nationalism to combat the unofficial nationalists, seeking loyalty for the state through an appeal to patriotism, expressed in state symbols such as the flag, army, and national anthem. This clash of nationalisms emphasises the pervading appeal which nationalism has in modern politics, and such conflict is in effect a form of international relations, but with only one side possessing full statehood (see Chapter 10 for further discussion of nationalism in international relations).

The nationalist movements which aim for total independence seek to destroy existing states, while other forms of political activity, even Marxist revolutionary movements, usually leave the boundaries of the state intact. Only the nationalists who fought for the establishment of independent states in place of the colonies left the existing boundaries alone. This often meant that later a new set of nationalists, representing the 'nations within the nation', came to press for self-government within or outside the newly independent states, for example, the Ibos in Nigeria who sought to establish the state of Biafra.

The apparently intractable and non-negotiable nature of the nationalist demand – national self-determination – makes nationalist political behaviour seem a different kind of political behaviour from that of any other, at least regarding the territorial integrity of the state. That is why it is so feared and resisted by state governments everywhere. Yet the reality is that there is a wide spectrum of demands within nationalism and nationalist politics, and a wide variety of modes of political behaviour, from terrorism to constitutional electioneering. The politics of nationalism is a complex interchange of forces both between nationalists and others, and between nationalists themselves (for this, see particularly Brass, 1985). Each plays for the support of the wider public, and each deploys its own resources and exploits its opportunities. The case studies which follow illustrate these political manoeuvrings and their results. Each can be analysed according to the general features involved. First, the resources generated by the nationalists themselves can be analysed: their ability to organise, to gain support, and to influence governments and international opinion. Here, the degree of division among the nationalists, involving perhaps several nationalist parties, nationalist organisations, terrorist organisations, etc, is relevant. The more divided they are, the more they can be resisted.

Second, the political context in which the nationalists operate ultimately determines their success or failure. Depending on the type of resistance they meet, nationalists may have to fight to the death for their aims, or they may face an 'open door', or any situation between the two. An authoritarian state may suppress nationalist movements while a liberal state will allow them free expression within the law. But even these categories can vary over time in the nature of their responses. In communist USSR, Stalin took a very different approach to the 'Nationality Question' from Gorbachev, and in liberal-democratic Britain Thatcher is unyielding on Scottish and Welsh devolution compared to Callaghan. Only the political histories of these countries can explain why such changes occurred.

So we have both a 'bottom-up' and a 'top-down' view of the politics of nationalism and ethnicity. In the former, the nationalists themselves provide the resources, but in the latter their capability is determined by the whole political environment in which they find themselves, especially the response of anti-nationalists at home and in the central government. What determines the 'variables' and the result of the interaction between these is the central question in this study. In the case studies, there will be discussion of these variables, and of the results of nationalist political behaviour. The complexity of each case means that the discussion is necessarily brief and simplified. No definite conclusions can be offered, rather an indication of the features which are related to the theoretical models introduced in this book.

6

Nationalism in the 'First World'

The following case-studies provide a brief discussion of contemporary nationalist and ethnic politics in different parts of the world. These are the cases which have been the most prominent in recent years, and are the most obvious tests of the theoretical models discussed in this book. Of course, many other cases could be discussed, as well as parts of the world where nationalism appears to be less prominent in politics. It would be desirable to cover all the cases in the world, for a general theory of nationalism should be comprehensive as well as comparative. However, the agenda for this book is already over-filled with the cases considered here. Other cases of nationalist movements must be assumed to share most of the features of those discussed here, but to lack the intensity of these features. Where nationalism seems to be barely present at all (an unlikely scenario) the 'necessary conditions' for nationalist politics as described here should be lacking.

Western Europe

Nationalism in Europe has revived generally since the 1960s, after a period of apparent quiescence in the aftermath of the Second World War. Nationalist parties or movements which have had a considerable, though variable, impact on contemporary west European politics are to be found in Britain (Scottish, Welsh, Irish, National Front, British National Party), France (Corsican, Breton, Occitan, National Front), Spain (Catalan, Basque, Galician), Belgium (Fleming, Walloon), Italy (S. Tyrolean), Switzerland (Jura), and Germany (Republican Party).

There is also a related political movement, 'regionalism', which can seem to shade into nationalism where linguistic or cultural characteristics define the region. Some writers treat nationalism and regionalism as the same subject (e.g., Keating, 1988), and it is certainly difficult to draw a line between them in some countries. Here, the case studies focus on explicitly nationalist movements, and exclude 'regionalisms' such as those of the Mezzogiorno in Italy and Andalusia in Spain. While this is to some extent a false distinction as far as the economic and territorial aspects of the subject are concerned, it is a real distinction when the cultural and ideological dimensions are considered. Regions are not nations, since they do not fulfil the necessary conditions for nationhood. In the same way, 'regionalism' is not 'nationalism'.

Is there any general explanation for the revival of nationalism in Europe? And what are the particular features of these nationalist movements? After the war, the map of Europe was drawn up by the Superpowers, and the principal political division was an ideological and military one, that between communism on the one hand and the capitalist West on the other. At that time, all the political, economic and cultural resources of the continent were fully occupied with recovery and with the conditions of the Cold War.

By the 1960s, recovery was well under way, and expectations were also changing, both about internal politics and about the international world. There was a higher degree of security, both economically and militarily, for most people, and this made room for the alternative politics of culture and consumerism. Democracy was extended to include greater participation, and more parties were formed, which picked up votes as older party alignments loosened. This opened the way for nationalist parties to enter elections in opposition to the state-centred parties.

At this time too, the state began to institute regional policies to try to redress the economic imbalances between the rich and poor parts of the country. These regional policies led to the establishment of government agencies within historic nations such as Scotland and Brittany, which fuelled expectations and increased the identity of these nations within the state structure, although that was not intended. However, such policies were largely unsuccessful, and nationalist parties were able to exploit their failure in redressing the territorial imbalances in the economy (Keating, 1988).

The post-1945 nationalist parties varied greatly in character and strength. The Scottish National Party, whose origins go back as far as 1928 but which had never won many votes, was one of first to be markedly successful in elections, winning 30% of the Scottish vote in the election of October 1974. The Welsh Nationalist Party (Plaid

Cymru) rose to 11.5% of the Welsh vote in 1970. Both of these parties dropped considerably in support thereafter, but the electoral threat to the major parties was sufficient to make them concede devolution to Scotland and Wales, although this was made subject to referendums in 1979 with a special rule that 40% of the electorate should vote Yes. In the event, this test was not passed in either nation, and in Wales there was a 4:1 vote against. Thus it appeared that the nationalist parties had failed to mobilise their nations, and that the central state had revealed the divisions therein, while appearing to concede to nationalist pressures.

In fact, the centre in Britain never really conceded much to nationalism, since the form of devolution offered retained most power in the capital. This was apparent to most at the time of the referendums, and contributed to the low turnout and Yes vote. The Scottish and Welsh cases show that the 'bottom-up' view of nationalist political behaviour applies well in the initial stages. A strong nationalist party with good electoral support will usually bring about concessions from the centre, but the centre will exercise its constitutional power and political ingenuity to confuse the nation and meet its demands only half-way. Thus 'top-down' politics prevails unless the pressures and resources from below are maintained or increased. In the case of Scotland and Wales, these pressures and resources largely evaporated for several years, to be revived again in the late 1980s. By this time, however, the Thatcher Conservative Government refused to concede anything to nationalism, and the nationalist pressures from below were largely contained. That is because the Opposition Labour Party was able to act in a nationalist fashion while gathering in its traditional class vote. Many Scots and Welsh voters hoped to get their socioeconomic and nationalist demands satisfied by supporting Labour, and believed they could deliver as the British Government. If that were not possible, however, the potential for increased Nationalist voting remained, and was already in evidence by 1988, when the SNP won the Glasgow Govan by-election from Labour.

The SNP and Plaid Cymru were unusual in the politics of nationalism in having succeeded in winning many votes in elections (though never a majority), and in being the only credible nationalist parties claiming to represent their nations. Only in Catalonia and in Euskadi (the Basque country) after 1975, and in the 'Nationalities' of the Soviet Union and Yugoslavia since 1989, have nationalist parties been more successful electorally. Popular support for nationalist parties in Catalonia and

Euskadi goes back to the late 19th century. Their electoral activities were interrupted by the Franco regime from 1939 to 1975, when they were proscribed. Even in Catalonia and Euskadi, however, the nationalists have been split into several parties, especially in the latter, where the moderate Basque Nationalist Party (PNV) is estranged from the more separatist Herri Batasuna (HB), and from the left-wing Euskadiko Eskerra (EE).

At the first Basque 'autonomous' (regional) election in March 1980, Basque nationalist parties won 64.2% of the vote, divided among four parties. The largest, the PNV, won 37.6%, followed by 16.3% for Herri Batasuna. The PNV won 43% of the vote in the 1984 Basque elections, HB 15%, and EE 8%. At the 1986 'autonomous' election, the PNV split, with Eusko Alkatasuna (EA), a right-wing splinter party, taking 15.9% of the vote. The PNV was reduced to 24% of the vote. In total, Basque parties won almost three-quarters of the vote in 1986, but the PNV was forced into a coalition with the Socialist Party in order to keep HB out of government. Nevertheless, the PNV has been the main governing party in Euskadi (Basque country) since 1980.

In Catalonia too, the nationalist Convergence and Unity Party (CiU) is the leading party in Catalan regional elections, increasing its vote in regional elections from 27.6% in 1980 to 47% in 1984 and 46% in 1988 to form the government of Catalonia. In Spanish elections, however, the PNV and CiU have done worse and the Socialists and Spanish parties better, which indicates that nationalist voting is lower in state-wide elections than in regional (national) elections. For a summary of these elections, see Tables 6.1 and 6.2.

Nationalist parties in other parts of western Europe have won fewer votes, and many have similarly had to compete with other nationalist parties representing a choice between total separation or autonomy, and between socialism, liberalism and conservatism. Obviously such a division weakens the nationalist cause, but success or failure in gaining concessions from the state is determined also by the intensity of the nationalism involved, and by the reaction of the centre. Nationalist voting makes the government of the state responsive if it is dependent on electoral support from its constituent nations, whether through state-wide parties with strong national wings, or when small nationalist parties hold the balance of power in central legislatures.

This introduces the whole picture of party politics in the state and in the nation. For it is not just the nationalist parties who determine the political agenda, though they may place the nation's claims on that

Table 6.1 *Catalan Elections*

| | Autonomous elections | | | | | | Spanish election | |
| | 1980 | | 1984 | | 1988 | | 1989 | |
	%	seats	%	seats	%	seats	%	seats
CiU	27.6	43	47.0	73	46.0	69	38.3	18
PSC–PSOE	22.4	33	30.3	40	30.0	42	32.1	20
AP/PP	2.4	-	7.7	11	5.4	6	11.0	4
ERC	8.9	14	4.4	5	4.2	6	3.2	-
PSUC	18.7	25	5.6	6	-	-	-	-
PCC	-	-	2.4	-	-	-	-	-
IC	-	-	-	-	7.8	9	5.3	3
CDS	-	-	-	-	3.9	3	3.9	1
Others	20.1	20	2.5	-	2.8	-	6.3	-

Key

CiU: (Convergence and Unity). Right-of-centre nationalist (led by Pujol).
PSC–PSOE: (Catalan-Spanish Socialists).
ERC: (Esquerra Republicana de Catalunya). Regionalist party.
PSUC: (Catalan Communists). Official Catalan branch of PCE (Spanish Communist Party).
IC: (Communist Left). Catalan version of IU (United Left).
AP/PP: (Popular Alliance).
CDS: (Democratic and Social Centre). Conservative Party.
PCC: (Catalan Communists). Dissident Communist Party.

agenda. The other parties must respond, and how they do so is crucial, since in all the cases mentioned here the nationalist parties by definition do not possess majority support or representation in the state.

State-wide parties may split into national wings under pressure from nationalism. In Belgium, the Socialist, Christian Social, and Liberal Parties split into Flemish and Walloon wings after 1965, and fought elections on their own platforms. This meant that nationalism could be expressed as much through them as through the nationalist parties, the Volksunie (Flemish Nationalists) and the Rassemblement Wallon (Walloon Nationalists). The nationalist parties were unable to muster more than a fifth of the vote in their nations, and peaked in the mid-1970s. This did not mean that nationalism declined in Belgium. Rather, the old parties took over the nationalist claims and proceeded to federalise Belgium along linguistic and national lines.

In Belgium the central government became highly responsive to national claims through the splits in the major parties and, after the

Table 6.2 *Basque country (Euskadi) elections*

	Autonomous elections						Spanish election	
	1980		1984		1988		1989	
	%	seats	%	seats	%	seats	%	seats
PNV	38.0	25	42.7	32	23.7	17	20.3	5
PSE–PSOE	14.0	9	25.3	19	22.0	19	22.1	6
HB	16.5	11	14.7	11	17.5	13	16.2	4
EA	-	-	-	-	15.9	13	11.4	2
EE	9.7	6	8.0	6	10.9	9	9.0	2
Coaln. P./AP	4.7	2	9.3	7	4.8	2	10.3	2
CDS	-	-	-	-	3.5	2	4.1	-
UCD	8.4	6	-	-	-	-	-	-
PCE	4.0	1	-	-	-	-	-	-
Others	4.0	-	-	-	1.7	-	6.5	-

Key

PNV: (Basque Nationalist Party). Moderate, centrist.
HB: (Herri Batasuna). Political wing of ETA (extreme nationalist).
PSE–PSOE: (Basque/Spanish Socialists).
EA: (Eusko Alkatasuna). Right-wing breakaway from PNV.
EE: (Euskadiko Ezkerra). Breakaway from Communist Party.
Coalition P./AP: (Coalicion Popular). Popular Alliance.
CDS: (Democratic and Social Centre). Conservative Party.
UCD: (Union of Christian Democrats). Conservative Party.

Note: I am grateful to Dr Paul Heywood of the University of Glasgow for supplying me with much of the above information.

constitutional changes, devolved powers to the national communities and regions (the distinction between the powers of communities and regions in Belgium is broadly between cultural and economic matters; in both cases the nations are the basis of the division, except for Brussels, which is bilingual and has a regional council only, cultural matters being shared between the French and Flemish Community Councils).

In Britain and France, the major parties did not split, but MPs and Deputies from the nations acted in a more nationalist or decentralist way. This evoked a governmental response, especially when left-wing parties were in office. The Labour Party in Britain and the Socialist Party in France became converted to decentralisation in the 1970s and introduced devolution legislation. In Britain the Labour Government was unable to achieve the qualified majority required to pass its schemes at referendums in Scotland and Wales in 1979.

In France, a general scheme of regional assemblies was introduced in 1982, with a special statute for Corsica, where nationalists had been extremely active. Brittany, however, was not given special treatment, perhaps because its nationalist activity had faded in the late 1970s. Its nationalist voting remained under 5%. In Corsica nationalist and 'autonomist' parties won around 15% of the vote in regional elections in the 1980s. The extreme nationalists (CCN) boycotted the first regional elections in 1982, but the autonomists (UPC) won 10.6% of the vote and 7 seats. Another nationalist party (PPC) won 2% of the vote, and one seat. In the 1984 regional elections in Corsica the nationalists (ex-CCN, now MCA) won 5% of the vote and 3 seats, as did the autonomists (UPC). Most voters continued to support the 'French' parties, and it was through these that nationalist and regionalist demands were channelled to Paris. Thus, unlike the position in Catalonia and the Basque Country, when regional elections were introduced to Corsica, the nationalists were unable to take control. Instead, the centre and right-wing parties reaped the benefit of nationalist pressure and Socialist reforms, and now also acted in a nationalist way on behalf of Corsica.

In Corsica, as in some other parts of Europe, there was a background of violent non-constitutional nationalism, expressed in bombings, kidnappings, killings, and robberies. Welsh language extremists, the IRA and UDA in Northern Ireland, ETA in the Basque country, and Swiss Jura separatists were also violent nationalists who posed a direct threat to the authority of the state. Extremist nationalism is probably the result of frustration with the effectiveness of constitutional methods, from the nationalist point of view. Where nationalists form a permanent minority, as in Northern Ireland, they have no hope of winning a majority in elections. Thus one source of legitimacy is denied them. They are also faced with intransigent central governments who resist the 'break-up' of the state. A political tradition of violence is invariably found in such areas, e.g., banditry in Corsica, and Fenianism and militant Orangeism in Ireland. In such a political culture, force seems a natural method to achieve political ends.

While violent nationalism hits the headlines throughout the world, it should be borne in mind that only a tiny minority of a nation indulges in such actions. But there may well be passive support from a much larger number, and the political impact is great. What the central state seeks to do is to eliminate the terrorists or to marginalise them by getting the support of the moderate nationalists. Thus in Northern Ireland, the British Government since 1974 has sought to defuse militant Irish nationalism by establishing a power-sharing 'Executive', including the constitutional nationalists (the Social and Democratic Labour Party). But when this Executive was set up in 1974, it was soon killed off by an Ulster Unionist backlash in another example of 'direct action', a general strike. Similarly, the Spanish state has had to support the moderate Basque National Party (PNV) against the extremist Herri Batasuna and the paramilitary ETA. Even so, the bombings continue, perhaps because HB and ETA have not shared in governmental power in Euskadi.

Contemporary European nationalism is peculiar in that it occurs in states which seemed to be well-established and stable. Most people by the 1950s had regarded Britain, France, Belgium and Spain as 'nation-states', rather than as 'multinational states'. It thus came as a big surprise when Scots, Welsh, Bretons, Flemings, Basques, and so on, came to voice nationalist demands, and to achieve a big political impact in the 1960s and afterwards.

Are there any general explanations for this? Inglehart has pointed to the changing political culture in advanced economies, or 'post-industrial societies', with popular support for 'post-materialist' values. He has shown that support for nationalist parties in Belgium in the early 1970s was heavily drawn from people with such values (Inglehart, 1977, pp. 234–43). Green Parties are also in favour of regional autonomy, with the Scottish Green Party supporting Scottish independence. At the same time, paradoxically, 'post-materialists' tend to favour supranational integration, for example in the European Community. What they do not show great affection for is the tradi-tional centralised state, nor the traditional class or religious parties. This can be termed a cultural explanation for nationalism, but it is also an explanation based on changes in the economic and international environment. In the case of Europe these changes had brought about a high standard of living and international peace and security, leading to less dependence on the state.

Despite these affluent conditions, nationalist movements express dis-content with the economic and political systems. They see their nations as disadvantaged economically within the state, and their political rights denied under an over-centralised constitution. Their success in altering these systems has been remarkable in recent years. For this we must look to *regime changes*, which have provided the opportunity for decen-tralisation policies. In Spain, the Franco regime, which had repressed the nations within Spain, was replaced by a democratic system in

1975, and it proceeded to introduce home rule. Democratisation and devolution in Spain were seen as two sides of the same coin. In France too, the advent of a new-style Socialist rule, after years of centralism of both right and left, opened the doors to regional devolution. In Belgium, the regime changed when the political parties split into Fleming and Walloon wings. This led on to constitutional reforms which split the government of the country on linguistic grounds. In Britain, the upsurge of Irish Republican nationalism in Northern Ireland was the result of a regime change. After 1968, the Northern Ireland Unionist Government of Terence O'Neill was forced into conceding civil rights to Catholics. This upset the status quo of Unionist domination, and opened the way for more virulent Nationalist activity. Then the British Government suspended the Stormont Parliament and Government in 1972, which created a constitutional vacuum in which Nationalists and Unionists turned increasingly to illegal, violent actions. In contrast, Scottish and Welsh nationalisms were rendered comparatively weak in the absence of a marked regime change. Devolution failed to go through, largely because the grassroots nationalist pressures were insufficiently strong to support it, and the centre remained relatively static. Thus in Britain a stalemate prevails, which leaves the demands of nationalism unsatisfied. This promises to be a growing political problem in the future. Elsewhere in Europe, the decentralisations of the 1970s and 1980s have largely satisfied moderate nationalist demands. It remains to be seen whether these changes will be stable, or will lead on to further demands and separation.

Quebec

Nationalism in Quebec has posed a major threat to the political system of Canada since the 1960s. The Parti Québécois (PQ), founded in 1968, won the Quebec Provincial election of 1976 with 41% of the vote and 71 out of 110 seats in the Quebec Assembly. It remained in office until 1985, when the Liberals were returned. In the meantime, the PQ had promoted its aim to make Quebec a separate state, on the formula of 'Sovereignty-Association', which meant that some links with the rest of Canada would be retained. However, even negotiations on the basis of this formula were rejected by the Quebec electorate in a referendum in 1980 by 59.5% to 40.5%, on an 84% turnout. Although the PQ was essentially the party of the French-speaking population, they were split equally between Yes and No (Fitzmaurice, 1985).

The case of Quebec shows that nationalist political behaviour can be a most unpredictable political force, although its foundations may be long-term. The French-speaking population of Canada, concentrated in Quebec, but also strong in 'Acadia' (New Brunswick) have always constituted a separate nation within Canada, and they rarely inter-married with the non-French speaking immigrants. Some, however, supported Canadian 'nationalism' and were Founding Fathers of the Confederation, so there was always some ambiguity as to which of the two nationalisms meant more to the francophone elites. The mass of the francophone population, however, felt itself to be the object of internal colonialism in a Canada dominated by English-speakers of British extraction. The Canadian Constitution in its federal structure (known in Canada as 'confederation' – the most decentralised form of federation) protected the francophone population with religious and linguistic guarantees. These were underwritten by the British Parliament until 'repatriation' of the Constitution in 1982.

What brought about the sudden rise of Quebec separatism in the 1960s, its equally sudden decline in the 1980s, and its revival in the 1990s, is still something of a mystery, even to Canadians. Many despaired of Canadian unity when the PQ achieved power, while the PQ in its turn was taken aback at its electoral defeats in the 1980 Referendum and in the Quebec election of 1985.

There is agreement among most observers that the rise of Quebec nationalism was largely the result of social and economic changes in Quebec in the 1960s: the 'Quiet Revolution'. This was a form of 'modernisation', with a growing urban economy and secularisation. The passivity of the French population under British rule, encouraged by the Catholic Church, came to an end, and a new generation asserted its civil rights, which included the right to national self-determination, the sole use of the French language in Quebec (including the English-dominated Montreal and suburbs), and control over the economy. Some Quebec nationalists in the Front pour la Liberation du Québec (FLQ) turned to violence, and in 1970 a Quebec government minister was murdered, and another kidnapped. This led to emergency powers being introduced in Quebec.

All these social and political developments can be considered a regime change, although they took place under the Quebec Liberal Party, which had indeed encouraged the 'Quiet Revolution'. The eclipse of the Liberals in 1974, and of the PQ in 1985, was the result of electoral choices which related as much to how these parties had governed as to any verdict on nationalism. The Liberals were tarnished by scandals in the 1960s and early 1970s; the PQ failed in economic mangagement when it was in power.

Regime changes also occurred at the centre which profoundly affec-ted the strength of nationalism in Quebec. Pierre Trudeau, the Lib-eral Prime Minister of Canada virtually continuously from 1968 to 1984, though a French-speaker from Quebec, was a Canadian 'official' nationalist who sought the unity of Canada through bilingualism and strong central power. His policies seemed to threaten Quebec, since bilingualism there could mean the weakening of the French language (Laponce, 1985), and centralisation was at odds with a Quebec inde-pendence. In this regime change then, Quebec nationalism flourished as a reaction to aggressive Canadian nationalism.

However, another regime change took place in 1982 when a new Constitution was introduced for Canada, the first 'repatriated' from Britain. Although Quebec's PQ Government refused to sign this, on the grounds that it did not respect Quebec's nationhood and threat-ened further centralisation, it was probably a step towards a looser federation. When Trudeau's Government was replaced by Mulroney's Progressive-Conservatives in 1984, the new Canadian Government made further concessions to Quebec, including recognising that 'it con-stitutes within Canada a distinct society', though not on the unilingual French basis introduced by the PQ in Quebec in the late 1970s. This formula was finally agreed by Quebec's new Liberal Government in 1987, in the 'Meech Lake Accord', and put out to ratification by the ten Provinces. It was rejected by the PQ and by Trudeau, now in Opposition, and two Provinces failed to ratify it by the deadline of June 1990.

This failure indicates the ambiguous nature of the settlement, which satisfied neither the Quebec nationalists nor the Canadian 'federalists'. In Quebec itself, a revival of 'separatism' occurred in 1989 when the PQ won 41% of the vote in the Provincial Elections, compared with 50% for the Liberals. The first-past-the-post electoral system, however, now penalised the PQ where it had benefited it in 1976, for it won only 29 seats to the Liberals' 92 seats. Support for separation rose to 28% in a July 1989 opinion poll, and to 53% in a poll in May 1990, the highest ever. The English-speakers in Quebec, for their part, remained unhappy, and many deserted the Liberals for the Equality Party, which won 4 seats on a platform of the protection of English language rights in the Province.

The revival of nationalism in 1989 was related to the establishment of a free trade area between Canada and the United States. This made the Canadian economy less important to Quebec than its links with the US (the same was true of the western Provinces). So there was an element of economic rationality in supporting an independent Quebec within a free trade area with the US. Quebec nationalists could assuage fears of economic isolation under independence, just as the Scottish Nationalists could with their slogan 'Independence in Europe'.

The Canadian system of government has been fundamentally changed to take account of moderate Quebec nationalism, represented by the Liberals. Yet Quebec remains within the Canadian federal structure and its unilingualism has been checked, if not overcome. Its national identity is now constitutionally recognised (if not finally ratified), but it is not clearly accepted by the English-speaking population. Canada is one state and two nations.

The lesson of this case for nationalist parties is that their electoral support can be highly volatile and dependent on the effect of the electoral system, even if the underlying nationalism is strong (it is not usually predominantly separatist, however). Other political parties can capitalise on nationalism and engineer regime changes which satisfy moderate nationalist feeling and keep the nationalist parties out of power. The PQ tried to take Quebec out of Canada, but failed to convince the Quebec electorate, let alone the rest of Canada. The defeat for nationalism which the 1980 Referendum seemed to represent resembled that sustained by the SNP and PC in Scotland and Wales in 1979. Quebec nationalism revived under the auspices of the Liberals in the 1980s, just as the Labour Party took over much of Scottish and some of Welsh nationalism in the same period. These cases show that the variable fortunes of nationalist parties may disguise a steady advance in nationalism in other parties.

At the same time, the nationalist parties can revive if they can demonstrate potential economic advantages of independence to the voters. The case of Quebec shows, contrary to Gellner and other theorists of modernisation, that ethnic differences can prevent the emergence of a 'nation-state', even under the conditions of an industrialised society and a long-established state. Modernisation within an ethnically-divided society may increase nationalism, and not just at the early stages of development, but in mature economies.

Ethnic Politics in the United States and Britain

'Ethnic politics' refers to the politics of 'ethnic groups' or 'ethnic minorities'. While a broad interpretation of ethnic group would include 'ethnic nation' as used earlier, the contemporary political usage is much narrower. In this context, ethnic groups or minorities do not usually possess a defined territory, and their aims differ from those of 'classical' nationalists in that they do not seek 'national self-determination' within a national territory. Rather, they seek protection and advancement for the group, and especially for individuals in the group, within an existing state. Only rarely do they form ethnic parties or secession movements. Instead they tend to work through pressure groups, community action associations, and established multiethnic political parties.

Members of such ethnic groups tend to be recent immigrants, or inhabitants of states with a special history of slavery, indenture, or forced migration. Thus in the United States, nineteenth century immigrants such as the Irish and Italians were typically engaged in ethnic politics. Today, Hispanics and Asians are beginning to occupy a similar position in some parts of the US. Blacks, most of whose forebears were slaves, straddle the categories 'ethnic' and 'race', but with no clear distinction other than that of skin colour. In Britain, 'ethnic minorities' are either black or Asian, with no distinction usually being made between the two.

Many other countries have different types of ethnic politics, such as politics relating to 'guest workers' in Germany, or to Moslems in France. It is also reasonable to include long-established pockets of minority populations as 'ethnic' rather than 'national' where no nationalist aims or viable nationalist movements have developed. Of course, this gives rise to the criticism that ethnic groups are really failed nations, since their credentials as nations have failed to be successfully established (Hobsbawm, 1990). Here, however, attention is focused on the 'non-nationalist' politics of ethnic groups.

Even so, ethnicity, race and nationalism are linked. Black African nationalism is found not only in Africa but also in the US and in Britain. While there are connections between the two, the contexts are of course different. In the US, social and political change after 1945, and especially after the Korean War, led to a strong civil rights movement, which achieved considerable success in the 1950s and 1960s, after a fierce struggle. In Britain, black immigration from the Caribbean and immigration from Asia (mainly India and Pakistan) produced similar pressures for civil rights when these groups became politically active in the 1960s.

These developments fit in with the features associated with the rise of nationalist movements generally, such as the political mobilisation of the nation at the grassroots and a 'regime change' at the top. In Britain and the US, the black and Asian populations gradually rose in social status and started to organise effectively; the government changed the constitutional and political system in response, thereby providing the opportunity for further political action.

There are links between black African nationalism and black nationalism in the US. The example of the newly independent black states in Africa was encouraging to oppressed blacks in America and Europe. In the US, many black nationalists see themselves today as 'Afro-Americans' and stress their roots in Africa. A few have even identified with Africa entirely, and have returned there. Most, however, assert their nationalism as US citizens, but they also support special black institutions such as black churches, schools, colleges and business firms. The extreme expression of black nationalism was the 'Black Power' movement, which in the 1960s spawned a violent wing, the Black Panthers. This made no progress in the 1970s, and by the 1980s Black nationalism was essentially constitutional in its methods.

Blacks in Britain (whose African origins are usually mediated by residence in the Caribbean islands) similarly assert their rights in terms of British citizenship. Their nationalism is mainly concerned with the promotion of black cultural identity in a 'multicultural' British society. There is hardly any Afro-British nationalism, nor has there been a Black Power movement in Britain.

Black nationalism in the US and Britain is related to the larger pattern of ethnic politics in these countries. Ethnic groups seek a variety of political objectives including 'civil rights' ('equal opportunity', or the abolition of adverse ethnic and 'racial' discrimination), advantages for their group ('positive discrimination'), and a share in party organisation and government (reserved places). It is clear these different strategies are not exactly consistent, either in philosophical or practical terms.

In the United States and Britain, 'race' and ethnicity are usually distinguished from one another, with the former label applied to 'blacks', 'browns' and 'yellows' of ultimate African and Asian origin, and the latter applied to other ethnic groups, usually European in origin. While there is little scientific basis for the distinction between race and ethnicity, the political distinction is a strong one, as we shall see.

'Race relations' in politics in practice means the relationship between citizens of different skin colours. 'Ethnic politics', on the other hand, conventionally concerns white or near-white ethnic groups of European origin in the US such as Irish, Italian, German, and Latin-Americans (Hispanics). These are not official or rigid distinctions, nor are they likely to be permanent in politics. For some writers, 'race' should be replaced by 'ethnic group' (Miles, 1982), and 'good race relations would be ethnic relations' (Banton, 1983, p. 397). The distinction made by Banton is that 'race' denotes an exclusive ethnic group based on colour, while an 'ethnic group' is a voluntary association based on beliefs about a common heritage. Ethnic competition is thus more open and acceptable to liberal thinkers than racial competition. It is of course very difficult (but maybe not impossible) to transform exclusive 'racial groups' based on colour into inclusive 'ethnic groups'. Nor is it always the case that ethnic groups are in practice inclusive (open to all).

Legislation on civil rights and race relations in the US and Britain is vague about who is covered, but the political intention is clear: to protect blacks and Asians from continuing white oppression and discrimination. This pinpoints the essential political difference between the 'politics of race' and 'ethnic politics'. Nearly all blacks in the US and Britain share a heritage of slavery. This dominates their political position to this day, and has largely determined their economic and social status. European, Asian, and Latin-American immigrants came as free citizens, and have experienced fewer difficulties in establishing a favourable economic and social status. Thus black politics is directed at redressing the legacy of slavery, and ethnic politics is about achieving gains for ethnic groups in what is for them a relatively open and competitive political system.

It is significant that only blacks have espoused nationalism along the lines of 'Black Nationalism'. That is because the channels of ethnic politics have been largely closed to blacks, on account of the background of slavery, and because of colour discrimination. The 'melting-pot' of the American nation has been quicker to melt the different (white) ethnic groups than it has been to melt the blacks with the whites. And since the 1960s it has largely ceased to melt the ethnic groups too, preferring to stress ethnicity along with equal citizenship in the 'American Dream' of the 'Land of the Free' (Glazer and Moynihan, 1975).

The 'melting-pot' was always an inept image where colour was concerned. There is no way that colour distinctions can be eliminated.

Non-colour ethnic distinctions can be changed or ignored, but this will only happen in certain circumstances. As in the other case-studies, we find here that ethnicity predominates as a political interest where class, religion, and territory are comparatively weak as social divisions. This condition has been found at various times in American and British political history.

The first manifestation of ethnic politics in the US and Britain was the organisation of immigrant groups by the political parties into voting blocs. Irish, Jewish, Italian, and German immigrants to the US in the 19th and early 20th centuries retained a strong ethnic identity as long as it was difficult for them to assimilate to the predominant 'Anglo-Saxon' American nation. And even when assimilation was possible, many preferred to continue to stress an ethnic identity in order to benefit from the political share-out of jobs and services. In the absence of a comprehensive merit system of recruitment to public employment, patronage was brokered by ethnic leaders, who in turn delivered the votes of the group to the party. Even today, American politicians make direct appeals to ethnic groups in order to win votes, and some residue of patronage along ethnic lines still persists.

In Britain, the 'Irish vote' and the 'Jewish vote' have historically occupied a similar position in the political system. These went to the Liberal and Labour Parties, for the Conservative Party primarily represented the Anglican and English establishment. Today, these ethnic groups vote much more according to social class, as the barriers to their social advancement have been reduced. Even so, Catholics are heavily skewed in their votes to the Labour Party, irrespective of class. This is not so much a matter of Irish ethnicity (a weak identity among many Catholics in Great Britain) as of political opportunism. The Labour Party offers an avenue to power for Catholics which is still not available in other parties. Jews, on the other hand, have largely deserted the Labour Party for the Conservatives as they have grown more prosperous, despite some anti-Semitism amongst right-wingers. Such views are outweighed by the ideological congruity between Thatcherism and the Jewish business ethnic, bolstered by the great economic success of many Jews in British society (Alderman, 1983, 1989).

Most attention in Britain is now paid to the 'black vote' and the 'Asian vote', which goes heavily to the Labour Party (Anwar, 1986). The political influence of that vote is not great, however, since the British political system does not encourage ethnic politics. That is because there is less pride in diverse ethnicity in Britain than in the

United States, for the country does not see itself as an immigrant nation. There is a more centralised and bureaucratised governmental structure in Britain, which leaves little room for patronage to ethnic groups such as at the level of state and local government in the US, where ethnic pressure is most easily wielded. The British party system is made up of parties of a predominantly class character, with ideological, not sectional, programmes.

The American party system, on the other hand, is decentralised and non-programmatic, and is in reality a coalition of numerous interests. In this system, there is easy access for ethnic groups, and a 'log-rolling' political process whereby groups support one another to get legislation passed in the interests of all of them. A disciplined party system, such as that in the British Parliament, does not allow for this.

The log-rolling process is not always possible when there are political conflicts between ethnic groups. Black groups are unable to cooperate with white racist groups such as the Ku Klux Klan and right-wing American groups which stress white interests. More complexly, Black nationalists and Jews have come into conflict for a variety of reasons. Although both Blacks and Jews engage in ethnic politics as historically disadvantaged groups, the present social and economic position of most Jews is well ahead of Blacks. In particular, Blacks are often in subordinate face-to-face situations with Jews, as tenants of Jewish landlords and as employees in Jewish shops and businesses. This emphasises a cultural division of labour between them.

An international dimension is also involved. Israel has ties with South Africa in trade and defence procurement which Blacks naturally object to. In addition, Black Moslems, who are a type of Black nationalist movement, side with their co-religionists in the Middle East against Israel. This is one example where domestic and international factors shape ethnic relations (see also Chapter 10).

The big question for ethnic groups in American and British politics is how far they should seek a separate identity and how far they should work within parties and organisations with a multi-ethnic or non-ethnic character. In both the US and Britain ethnic parties have been almost totally absent, although an Islamic Party of Britain was formed in 1989 to represent the peculiar interests of Moslems held to be neglected by the other parties. Instead, Blacks have sought a political role in the mainstream political process, including direct representation in non-ethnic parties. Thus, the Labour Party was faced with a demand for a 'Black Section' in the late 1980s. This was rejected in 1988, yet an affiliated 'Black Socialist Society' was granted in 1990. This did not satisfy the advocates of formal Black Sections.

In the US, ethnic groups work through the Democratic and Republican parties. The constitutional structure inhibits the establishment of minor parties generally but, as we have seen, a more fundamental reason for the absence of ethnic parties is the relatively open nature of the major parties to pressure groups, especially at the state and local government level. There are now many black mayors of American cities, usually Democrats, and ethnic groups play a large part in state politics. In Congress, however, blacks are a tiny group, and statewide elections for the Senate favour 'White Anglo-Saxon Protestant' ('WASP') candidates over 'ethnic' candidates. That is because it is impossible for any one ethnic group to carry the election over such a wide territorial area. When an ethnic candidate is put up, the other ethnic group voters tend to prefer a 'WASP' as more neutral and more 'American'. In a presidential election especially, a 'Bush' has an advantage over a 'Dukakis'.

Despite this, there has been a revival of ethnicity and ethnic politics in the US, and signs of increased ethnic political activity in Britain too. Why is this? Black political activism in both countries spearheaded the new consciousness of ethnicity. The response of the state in the US and Britain was to concede 'civil rights' and in the US 'positive discrimination' through quotas for blacks in education and public employment. This legitimation of ethnicity encouraged other ethnic groups to follow the Blacks in their search for roots, their new-found ethnic pride, and their political activism (Martin Kilson in Glazer and Moynihan, 1975). So ethnic politics revived as a channel of influence in American and British democracy after a period of quiescence since the first wave of mass immigration ended in 1924 in the US and in 1914 in Britain (mainly Irish and Jewish). Since the 1950s, 'Black' (Caribbean and Asian) immigration to Britain produced the pressures for civil rights which the long-established Black population produced in the US in the 1950s and 1960s. The later (from the 1970s) mass migration to the US of Hispanics from Latin America and of Asians from Indo-China and the Philippines has added a new dimension to US ethnic politics.

The successes of Black politics in the US in the 1960s produced a reaction among whites in the 1970s and 1980s, pushing them towards the Republican Party. In Britain too, many white voters in the working class turned away from the Labour Party to support the Conservative Party in areas such as London and the West Midlands of England where Blacks and Asians were numerically strong and politically influential in the Labour Party. The Conservative Party has been careful to avoid an overt appeal to white racism, and Enoch Powell's and Norman Tebbit's anti-immigrant stance was officially renounced. Nevertheless, both Labour and Conservative Governments passed a series of laws to restrict 'New Commonwealth' (black) immigration from 1962 onwards. This was in contrast to the liberalisation of US immigration laws at that time. In the US, the strict quotas imposed on non-European immigrants since the Chinese Exclusion Act of 1882 were relaxed in 1965, when civil rights legislation made discrimination on account of colour embarrassing in the context of immigration controls.

In Britain, there has been some working class support for the extreme 'nationalist' politics of the National Front and the British National Party, but these parties have made negligible gains in electoral terms, and the National Front did not contest any seats in the 1987 general election. National Front activists cause considerable communal tension and some violence, and the more general urban violence in British and American cities since the 1960s has contributed to the political polarisation between urban whites and blacks.

The failure of the Labour Party to keep much of its white working class vote in London and the areas of England with a strong Black or Asian immigrant population is partly the result of the Party's local identification with that population. This has repelled working class whites who fear a Black presence in housing, education, and employment as a threat to their economic position. There are thus clear 'class' reasons for racism in Britain (Miles, 1982).

Despite anti-immigrant 'white politics' in the Conservative Party, many Asians are attracted to it as the party which best represents the strong shopkeeping interest in the Asian community. Private education is popular with Asians who can afford it, on account of their religious preference for single sex schools and their intense desire to obtain top educational qualifications. All this draws them away from the Labour Party to the more middle class and private enterprise-oriented Conservative Party. So that Party has to satisfy both 'white' and Asian ethnic political pressures. In practice, it does this by officially avoiding ethnic issues in its election campaigns, concentrating instead on individualism and enterprise. On the ground, however, the politics of racism is important in sustaining the Conservative vote in some parts of Britain, and some Conservative candidates play on this.

Ethnic politics are more important in the US and Britain today than they were a generation ago. That is first of all because of the political successes of Blacks under the American civil rights legislation of the 1960s, leading to increased ethnic awareness in other groups. In Britain, mass immigration from the New Commonwealth in the 1950s and 1960s produced similar pressures for civil rights legislation and multicultural education. There followed a reaction in Britain in the form of immigration controls and racism.

The political culture of the US is more favourable to ethnic politics than that of Britain. Britain is also less receptive to multiculturalism, seeing itself not as a 'melting-pot' of immigrants, but as an old-established 'nation-state' essentially English in character. The inappropriateness of this for the increasing non-English, non-white population of Britain has led to the development of ethnic politics since the 1960s, but the satisfying of ethnic demands in Britain seems likely to continue to be more difficult than in the US for cultural and political reasons.

7

Nationalism in the 'Second World'

Perhaps the biggest surprise for students of nationalism in recent years has been the sudden upsurge of ethnic nationalism in communist states, especially in the Soviet Union and Yugoslavia. In the space of a few years, nationalist movements have arisen in several areas, and considerable ethnic violence has occurred. All this seems incompatible with the philosophy and practice of communism, in which nationalism is supposed to disappear, to be replaced by patriotism and 'proletarian internationalism' (see Connor, 1984). The complexities of Marxism need not detain us here, but the failure of Marxism to understand nationalism is significant. Marx and Engels predicted that national boundaries would, like the state, under socialism wither away, to be replaced by the solidarity across the nations of working people. Lenin espoused the doctrine of national self-determination when nationalism appeared to be stronger than socialism in defeating the Russian Empire. Once established, the Soviet Union was to suppress the nationalist movements within it which were seeking independence from Russia, but it did grant a sort of federal system with republics constituted along the lines of 'nationality'. National liberation movements abroad were supported wherever capitalist empires were the object of attack. Stalin espoused 'socialism in one country' as against Trotsky's internationalism and the 'Austro–Marxist' (e.g., Rosa Luxemburg) view of nationality as pertaining to individuals and not to territory (Hobsbawm, 1990, pp. 7, 33). This soon developed into 'Great Russian Chauvinism'. Many western political scientists in the past were prepared to follow the official view of the communist governments that they had indeed solved the 'Nationality Problem', or at least had harnessed it in a way which was supportive of the communist system (e.g., McAuley, in Harding (ed.), 1984). By the end of the 1980s, a completely new picture was emerging.

The USSR

In the USSR, several of the Soviet Republics were in turmoil with nationalist demands for independence, mass demonstrations, rioting, violence, bloodshed and deaths. The troubles ranged geographically from the Asian Republics such as Kazakhstan and Uzbekistan, the Caucasus (Armenia, Azerbaijan, Georgia) and Moldavia near the Black Sea, to the Baltic Sea (Estonia, Latvia, Lithuania). While these areas might be considered peripheral regions of the USSR, the appearance of a Popular Front in the Ukraine coupled with mass demonstrations in support of the Uniate Catholic Church there marked a spreading of nationalist sentiment to a core Republic. The Russians themselves were affected by nationalism, and reacted against the claims of the 'nationalities' (Russians are not considered officially to be a 'nationality' themselves). Organisations such as Pamyat (Memory) and Interfront were formed by Russians, the former including anti-Semitic elements, and the latter aiming to protect ethnic Russian interests in the non-Russian republics. In June 1990, the Russian Republic declared its 'sovereignty' within the Soviet Union, following the example of nearly all the other Republics.

What explanations can be given for this type of nationalist behaviour? There is something in common between these nationalisms and the ones discussed in the previous section. They have all arisen in the context of old-established states, which had already experienced nationalism since at least the 18th century, but which had apparently achieved political stability by the 1950s. However, the political systems differed greatly, with liberal democracy and free elections being the context for the western European nationalisms (except Spain before 1975), and communist authoritarianism the basis of the Soviet and Yugoslav systems. Moreover, it would be difficult to point to a 'post-industrial' political culture as contributing to the latter nationalisms, as shortages rather than affluence marked their economies. Yet it could be said that expectations were rising there too, particularly as regards civil rights, and that this resembles the 'post-materialism' in the west which contributed to nationalist political behaviour.

One obvious feature in common is that regime change seems to be the most important factor in explaining the sudden rise of nationalism in the USSR and Yugoslavia. Under the leadership of Mikhail Gorbachev, the USSR since 1985 has embarked on a profound change in its political system, encapsulated in the words *perestroika* (reconstruction) and *glasnost* (openness) (Gorbachev, 1988). Included in this change is a new freedom to express political views and to participate in the political system in organisations competing with the Communist Party. This has permitted nationalist political behaviour where previously it was repressed. In particular, it has allowed the election of nationalist politicians in competition with the official Communists (CPSU), and in some cases (e.g., the Baltic nations) the election of nationalist or nationalist-supported governments. These have asserted the right of secession granted in the Soviet Constitution. A throwback to the philosophy of Lenin and Stalin with its proclamation of the right of national self-determination, this clause in the Soviet Constitution was now activated by several nationalities under Gorbachev. However, the Soviet President resisted the implementation of this right by insisting on procedures for secession which would effectively veto it except on terms dictated by Moscow. Thus national self-determination for the constituent nations of the Soviet Union was to involve the consent of the Soviet Union as whole.

Glasnost has led to a revision of the official history of the Soviet Union. For example, the Nazi–Soviet Pact of 1939, which included the plan of annexation to the USSR of Estonia, Latvia, Lithuania, and Moldavia, was officially revealed in 1989. This led to commemorative nationalist protests in the annexed Republics. One such demonstration in the Baltic Republics in August 1989 was reported to have involved about two million people linking hands between the three Baltic capitals. Soon nationalist demonstrations in Moldavia, Armenia, Georgia and the Ukraine attracted the support of hundreds of thousands.

Perestroika means the reconstruction of the economic, constitutional, and political structure of the Soviet state, including the position of the 'nationalities'. The Soviet Union's Constitution already recognised these nationalities in its federal system of 15 Republics and various 'autonomous regions', which were based on national identities. But these Republics and regions were subject to Communist Party 'democratic centralism', which meant that no real autonomy existed. These territorial political units did, however, provide a formal structure of government for the nationalities, and a system of political and economic preferment for local elites within their Republics. This was to prove an essential resource for nationalism under Gorbachev's more open regime, for local Party leaders whose powers had been curtailed under the centralising rule of Yuriy Andropov (1982–4) were eager to reassert their authority under Mikhail Gorbachev.

Gorbachev was primarily concerned to reform the overall Soviet system with a view to increasing economic efficiency, but his programme also included greater decentralisation, especially in economic and budgetary matters (Gorbachev, 1988, p. 299). He probably did not expect that his new regime would unleash a series of ethnic disorders and nationalist claims, yet he could not easily repress these under *glasnost*. He no doubt hoped to harness popular energies for his reforms by giving greater independence to the nationalities, and he put nationalistically-inclined Party leaders into positions of power where they appeared to be reformers. In his clean-out of the 'old guard' he also cleaned out many wedded to the old ideas of centralism. Thus many Communist Party leaders in the Baltic Republics were new appointments who showed a sensitivity towards the nationalist demands of the Popular Fronts. In Lithuania, some of them broke away from the CPSU in December 1989 to form an independent Lithuanian Communist Party.

In other parts of the Soviet Union, Gorbachev's modernising appointments offended the local nationalists. In Kazakhstan, the local party leader was sacked in 1986 and replaced by a Russian. This provoked Kazakh nationalist rioting. Gorbachev's appointments were not designed to produce nationalism, rather to produce economic reforms. But the effect was to stimulate nationalism generally.

This gave an opportunity for nationalists who were more akin to those in the West to express themselves and be elected to office. While the new Gorbachev regime tolerated this, it opposed the breakaway of the Lithuanian Communist Party from the CPSU, and the declaration of independence by the Lithuanian Parliament at the end of 1989. He similarly denounced Latvia's and Estonia's declarations of independence in 1990. At the same time, he upheld the constitutional right of the republics to secede, although only on terms laid down by the USSR Constitution and implemented by the Soviet authorities. As the Baltic governments now rejected the legitimacy of this Constitution, conflict was inevitable. Economic sanctions were imposed on Lithuania, which retaliated with economic sanctions against Russia.

Two features of the conflict between the USSR and the Baltic nations were particularly difficult to resolve. One was military. The Baltic region is important for the Soviet armed forces, and independence for the Baltic nations threatened the security of the USSR. The army was also worried about desertions of non-Russian personnel, which could spread to other nationalities. The other difficult feature was the strong presence of Russians in the Baltic countries, especially in Latvia, representing their social and economic interdependence with the USSR. Russians manned many factories in Latvia, which were geared to serving the Soviet economy, having been financed by Moscow.

Here were strong features of 'internal colonialism' and a 'cultural division of labour', leading to 'anti-colonial nationalism'. As an 'imperial' power, the USSR was not prepared to lose its territory without a struggle, and in the absence of official support from the centre the 'nationalities' were in a weak position. Moreover, other states were not inclined to aid the break-up of the USSR if this jeopardised the improvement in east–west relations which had already led to the liberation of the eastern European nations. So the conditions in international relations were not ripe for a new state settlement involving the loss of territory for the USSR, especially as German unification within the western orbit was already threatening to tilt the balance of power against the Soviet Union.

It was not clear how many people in the Soviet nationalities sought total independence, however, though many (perhaps a majority) in the Baltic Republics voiced separatist sentiments. The governments of the more nationalistically-inclined Republics varied in their tactics to achieve independence. Some, such as Lithuania, appeared impatient, while others, such as Latvia and Estonia, seemed to be prepared to compromise on independence in the short-term. Moscow laid down that referendums on independence should be held, with at least two-thirds of the electorate in agreement. If Russians were included in the electorates of the Baltic countries (particularly Latvia and Estonia where they are numerous), then independence might not be carried. 'Ethnic nationalism' entered in when Latvian and Estonian Congresses were set up in 1990, elected by the citizens and their children of Latvia and Estonia in 1940. This electorate excluded later Russian and other immigrants. However, the full franchise Supreme Councils were the most important bodies, and were dominated by nationalists and members supported by them. Generalisations about nationalism in the Soviet Union are difficult to make, because of the considerable differences between the nations, between their nationalist movements, and between their relationships with the USSR.

Economic autonomy and the right to make the national language official was generally granted to the Republics in 1989. While Republican national flags and anthems were banned until Gorbachev, education in the native languages was never eliminated. It is true that a Russification campaign was continued from Tsarist times, under the banner of 'Soviet patriotism' and communist solidarity, but education in non-Russian languages was never stopped, and many spoke these languages at home, if not at work (Motyl, 1987). The result was that when Gorbachev opened up the Soviet system to nationalist demands, language and religion became a focus for nationalism in the politics of the Republics. In Estonia Russians went on strike in 1989 in protest against proposed voting qualification laws which would discriminate against them on grounds of length of residence. No doubt they were encouraged to do so by some centrist elements in the Communist Party, and Moscow declared the law unconstitutional.

The national conflicts are not just between the non-Russians and the Russians. They are also between the nationalities themselves. A bitter struggle erupted in 1988 between Armenians and Azeris over the region of Nagorno–Karabakh, an Armenian enclave in the Azerbaijan Republic, which had been allocated to Azerbaijan in 1923. Armenia demanded the incorporation of this region into Armenia, while Azerbaijan refused. Considerable violence broke out in both Republics with many deaths in Azerbaijan. Azerbaijan set up a commercial blockade to put pressure on Armenia. Moscow intervened to restore order and refused to sanction any boundary change. Instead, in 1989 it introduced 'direct rule' from Moscow over the Nagorno–Karabakh region, in the manner of British direct rule in Northern Ireland since 1972, and Indian direct rule in Punjab in 1987. At the end of 1989 Moscow restored the region to Azerbaijan. It seemed to be just as unable to pacify the nationalists on both sides as the British and Indian Governments with their direct rule.

Other inter-ethnic conflicts erupted in 1989 in Georgia between Abkhazis and Georgians, and in Moldavia between Moldavians, Ukrainians and Russians. A feature of these conflicts is that the rise of one nationalism usually produces a reaction from others. Georgian nationalists, under the virtual mandate given them by Gorbachev's policy of increasing the power of the national Republics, proceeded to promote the idea of the ethnic unity of Georgia and to play down the contribution of other ethnic groups to Georgian culture and history. They aimed to make Georgian the official language, and to extend the Tblisi State University into the non-Georgian region of Abkhazia. This provoked a violent nationalist response from the Abkhazis, whose language and culture is distinct from the Georgian. Thus the price of unleashing Georgian nationalism under *perestroika* has been to upset the balance between the Georgians and the non-Georgians. This type of situation is common throughout the world, where one nationalist upsurge begets another, either in imitation or in reaction.

In many of these cases too there is again present a cultural division of labour, with ethnic groups differentially placed in the labour market. But this time the 'core nation' may play no part, and internal colonialism is absent. Armenians typically engage in profitable trading in Azerbaijan. This gives rise to resentments, expressed for the first time openly as nationalism in the conditions of *glasnost*. But the Russians and the Soviet state are not directly involved in this cultural division of labour.

The form nationalism takes varies with the type of political culture. Mass demonstrations and violence erupts in areas where participative institutions are weakest; more sophisticated areas with a history of self-rule such as the Baltic Republics tend towards constitutional action, although they too have seen huge crowds demonstrating and 'illegal' declarations of independence, followed by economic and military sanctions.

The presence of long-standing religious animosities affects nationalist behaviour. Moslem–Christian divisions correspond to national divisions in many areas of the Soviet Union, as for example Azeri–Armenian and Abkhazi–Georgian. Shia Moslems everywhere have become more militant since the Iranian Revolution of 1979, and this has affected Soviet Moslems too, exacerbating ethnic and linguistic conflicts. Religious differences in the Baltic nations, in contrast, are not as extreme as these, but are important, with Catholic Lithuanians and Lutheran Latvians and Estonians in opposition to Russian Orthodox. So there is a strong cultural input into the different nationalisms of the Soviet Republics.

Although cultural nationalism was acceptable to Moscow, up to a point, secession and the redrawing of boundaries were ruled out, as were laws discriminating against non-nationals. Moscow ruled in 1989 that the unity of the Communist Party of the Soviet Union must be maintained, although the Lithuanian Party later seceded. It also laid down that the Russian language must be given equal status with the national languages as the official language of the Republics.

The clash between nationalists and the centre was perhaps the most difficult problem facing Gorbachev, and threatened either a break-up of the Soviet Union or the repression of the nationalist movements. A further regime change, this time in the direction of a reaction towards centralisation and authoritarianism, would make it very difficult, if not impossible, for nationalist politics to survive as long as the political and military elites stayed loyal to the centre.

It can be seen that in the USSR the 'top–down' explanation for the capacity for political nationalism seems to be the most important. Without a regime change at the top, nationalism could not be expressed in politics, as the system until 1985 was authoritarian and repressed overt nationalist behaviour. The limits to nationalism in the USSR are set by the Communist Party at the centre.

But next in importance is the scale and intensity of the 'bottom-up' nationalist behaviour, once it was allowed to express itself. That such nationalism gathered a very wide social spectrum of support, even surpassing Western nationalist movements, indicates that authoritarian political regimes can suppress nationalism but cannot eliminate it.

The explanation for this 'bottom–up' nationalism is to be found partly in the 'internal colonialism' of the Soviet state, with its strong 'cultural division of labour'. In particular, Russians are claimed by non-Russian nationalists to be exploiting them through centralised planning and forced industrialisation, which takes their resources away and gives them to the rest of the country. This takes the form of the introduction of heavy industry in some areas and the extraction of primary resources in others. The purpose is to serve the interests of other parts of the country, and it often damages the environment and economy of the nationalities. Russians migrate to get employment in the better-off Baltic Republics, and often take the best jobs. Migration threatens the ethnic balance of the population, with Latvians comprising only half of the population of Latvia. Russians, in reply, resent subsidising the poorer Nationalities in the Soviet Union, and many seek independence for themselves. Sudden or extensive changes in an economic system often lead to nationalism if these changes can be associated with differential economic gains for different ethnic groups.

As important as the economic explanation for nationalism is the political and cultural dimension. Political mobilisation occurred when elections became free and nationalists could compete openly with the Communist Party. The cultural aspects were clearly manifested in linguistic nationalism, national religion, and in the numerous symbols of the nation such as the flag, national anthem, dress, myths of history, etc. All these were to come together in Gorbachev's regime change, which provided the crucial opportunity for their expression.

Yugoslavia

Some of these features are also found in Yugoslavia, where until the death of Tito in 1980 the regime was largely authoritarian, especially with regard to separatist nationalist aspirations. After Tito, the leadership of Yugoslavia became much weaker, with a collective Presidency consisting of one representative each of the six Republics and two Autonomous Provinces. The Chairman is taken from each in turn. Each Republic and Province has a veto in the federal decision-making processs, and many economic functions are devolved to them and to self-managing enterprises, leaving the central government economically weak. Even before the death of Tito, the 1974 Constitution had established most of this decentralisation, and so provided a framework for nationalist activity once the restraint of Tito's power was removed. One of the 1974 changes was to remove the Province of Kosovo from the control of the Republic of Serbia, except for some residuary powers. This was to prove a major cause of nationalist conflict between the Albanians and Serbs in the 1980s. Thus regime change in Yugoslavia also provides a key explanation to the upsurge in nationalism.

But why was nationalism apparently waiting to arise, when the opportunity was given? For this, we must return to 'bottom–up' explanations which have proved useful in other case-studies. First, an economic explanation. Nationalism feeds on economic discontent, and channels it into a nationalist perspective. It does this especially when there is regional uneven economic development, and where there is a cultural division of labour and many immigrant workers. Both the Soviet Union and Yugoslavia are economies in dire trouble with shortages, uneven development and a strong tinge of 'internal colonialism'.

Then again there is a cultural explanation for nationalist behaviour. Each nation in Yugoslavia claims either a language, or a culture, and often a religion, and certainly a historic memory, which years of communist rule have failed to eliminate, and may have actually encouraged. Just how these relate to national identity and nationalism is extremely complex and ever-changing (Banac, 1984). In Yugoslavia, the competing national ideologies of the Serbs, Croats, and Slovenes were present from the foundation of the Yugoslav state in the 1920s, and continued to cause division under the communist regime. In particular, the 'Greater Serbian' nationalism is centralising and intolerant of the other nationalisms in Yugoslavia.

As in the Soviet Union, language differences have always been accepted and encouraged in Yugoslavia, up to a point. There is no one official Yugoslav language, and Serbo-Croat, Slovene, and Macedonian are recognised as official and equal languages, with minor languages regarded as equal in the Regions in which they are used. However, Croats do not always wish to be joined linguistically to Serbs, and Serbs and Albanians have fought bitterly over their respective rights in the Autonomous Province of Kosovo, part of the Republic of Serbia.

It was Kosovo which, in the most recent period, first showed that nationalism had re-emerged in Yugoslavia as a major political problem. From the start of the 1980s, the ethnic Albanians who make up a majority of the province demonstrated for greater autonomy, with some desiring incorporation with Albania. By 1988, the minority Serbian population had mobilised in reaction, and had found a champion in Serbia's party leader, Slobodan Milosevic, who demanded the total incorporation of Kosovo in Serbia. The issue was marked by violence, strikes and deaths in Kosovo, and threatened to break up the federation. It was compounded by the reaction of the other Republics, who fear the dominance of Serbia, which accounts for 40% of the total population. Slovenia and Croatia in particular voiced dissent against Serbia in the Central Committee of the federal Party in 1989, and sought greater independence in the federation. The Slovenian Communist Party Central Committee pressed for constitutional changes which would give Slovenia the right to secede from the federation, a claim rejected by the Yugoslav Presidency, even though the Slovenian leaders at first said that they had no intention to exercise the right. However, in 1990 the Slovenian Communist Party seceded from the Yugoslav party, and took up a more separatist stance. The reason for this change is that elections in Slovenia had made the politicians more responsive to nationalism, if they hoped to be elected. It was also apparent to Slovenians that Serbia was moving in a 'Greater Serbian' direction, which threatened the interests of Slovenia. Thus independence looked a more attractive proposition, especially in a changing eastern Europe of non-communist states linked to the European Community. Despite these last-minute moves by the Communists to satisfy nationalist opinion, multi-party elections in Slovenia and Croatia in April and May 1990 resulted in the election of non-communist, nationalistically-inclined Governments. These proceeded to declare themselves in favour of virtual independence for Slovenia and Croatia, a course of action hotly contested by the Yugoslav Presidency, now virtually unrepresentative of the Republics concerned.

While these national questions in Yugoslavia have a long history, their intensification in the 1980s and 1990s is thus the result of recent developments. The 1974 constitutional changes and the death of Tito in 1980 have already been mentioned. Failures in the Yugoslav economy became severe in the 1980s, and their effects were unevenly felt. At one end of the scale, Kosovo is one of the poorest parts of the country, while at the other end, Slovenia and Croatia are the richest. These differences are relatively large when compared to those in the States of the European Community.

Uneven regional development, coupled with corresponding cultural divisions, provided fertile ground for nationalism. The constitutional structure and the political culture determine the form which that nationalism will take. The nationalism of Slovenia and Croatia is linked to the demand for greater democratisation and liberalisation, while that of Kosovo is based on ethnic exclusiveness. Serbia's harks back to its historic dominance of the state ('Greater Serbia').

The power of the centre to resist these nationalisms is peculiarly weak in Yugoslavia, with little in the way of 'official nationalism', especially in the absence of the charismatic leader, Tito, and his control of the army. The state holds together through a form of consociationalism, whose tensions seem to be greater than such a system can bear. The introduction of multi-party elections in 1990 was the crucial 'regime change' which allowed non-communist, nationalist governments to be elected to power in Slovenia and Croatia. These aimed at some form of independence for these nations. This 'Balkanisation' is unattractive to Communist politicians and central economic interests, especially in Serbia. Moreover, the small successor states to Yugoslavia would not likely gain admission to the European Community, at least in the short run. Thus important elite groups in Yugoslavia remain committed to the continuation of the federation.

8

Nationalism in the 'Third World', South Africa, and the Middle East

The 'Third World' is usually considered to consist of most of Africa, Asia, and Latin America. In this area, economies are not as 'developed' as those of the First and Second Worlds, with a predominance of agriculture and relative poverty and debt. In politics, many states are relatively recent in origin, having gained independence from the Empires of the European powers. Nationalism and ethnicity take on a different form there from the rest of the world, although there are general features in common. Included in this chapter are accounts of nationalism in South Africa and in the Middle East. These areas are within the Third World geographically, but their economies and societies are more developed. In South Africa, the ideology and politics of apartheid have dominated in recent times, while in the Middle East in the same period (i.e., since 1948) the state of Israel has put into effect the ideology of Zionism. These cases are to a large extent *sui generis*, but there are many 'Third World' features in South Africa and Israel, and in the Middle East generally. The position of the Palestinians is somewhat similar to that of the Blacks in South Africa, and beyond that to many national groups in the Third World. So too is the form of nationalism found there.

The peculiarly vicious character of nationalism in this area is difficult to explain in terms of any of the theories which have been discussed so far. These theories deal with the causes of nationalism, but they do not accurately predict the form which that nationalism will take. It is only when the political culture of each area is taken into account, along with the unique unfolding of events, that a more complete explanation for such nationalist behaviour can be given. The exceptional violence in nationalist behaviour in much of Asia and Africa is consistent with the violent political culture in these continents. Bloodshed in politics is no stranger there, and the reasons for this lie in the history and social structure of the area. As Horowitz has pointed out in his study of ethnic groups in conflict (Horowitz, 1985, pp. 18–21), the reasons why ethnic conflict pervades Third World countries and takes a much more violent form there include (a) the relative absence of overarching identities with the state, which transcend or compete with those felt for the ethnic group, and (b) the absence of strong alternative identities within the ethnic group, e.g., class, religion, and language, which might form the basis of political action in non-ethnic parties and organisations. Instead, ethnic politics is the norm, and these factors together have produced a higher intensity of ethnic conflict than in the developed countries of the West. Finally, where the State habitually uses violence, ethnic groups have little alternative but to reply in kind.

Sri Lanka and the Indian Sub-continent

During the 1980s and into the 1990s, ethnic violence in Sri Lanka and in the Indian sub-continent claimed many thousand lives. This violence is not just the result of terrorism waged by extremist organisations. It is a much more widespread intercommunal conflict in which nationalist behaviour verges on genocide.

The first nationalisms in the Third World took the form of anti-imperialist movements. The Indian National Congress, founded in 1885, finally succeeded in ending British rule in India in 1947. However, the divide between Hindus and Moslems led to two states – India and Pakistan – being established, which was a defeat for Indian nationalism. Anti-British nationalism was soon to be succeeded by rival nationalisms within the sub-continent. Moslem identity proved unsuccessful in holding together the two separated parts of Pakistan, East and West. Instead, linguistic and territorial conflicts with West Pakistan led East Pakistan to secede in 1971, and to fight its way to independence with Indian aid as Bangladesh. In Kashmir too, the Moslems were split between India and Pakistan. This has given rise to Kasmiri (Moslem) nationalism, which has split between those supporting union with Pakistan and those seeking an independent state of Kashmir.

Ceylon, a separate British colony, became independent in 1948 and was renamed Sri Lanka in 1972, an indication that its official national identity was to be Sinhalese, despite the existence of a Tamil minority of around one-fifth of the population. Sinhalese nationalism produced reactive Tamil nationalism, resulting in civil war. Other nationalist movements in the sub-continent with a high level of violent behaviour are those of Sikhs (over 2,000 deaths in 1988) who seek to establish an independent Sikh state called Khalistan out of the Indian state of Punjab; the Gurkha National Liberation Front which seeks a separate state in Indian Bengal; and the Tripura National Volunteers in north-east India. These are only some of the more 'nationalist' organisations with well-defined claims to self-determination.

In addition, India and Pakistan are plagued by ethnic violence of a communal rather than nationalist kind, labelled variously 'tribal', 'sectarian' or 'caste'. Such conflict occurs in cities with changing immigrant populations such as Karachi and Hyderabad in Pakistan, and in rural areas where the caste system prevails. In the cities, migrant labour competes for jobs and housing with the indigenous population, and ethnic divisions become class divisions in a cultural division of labour. Caste systems are more rigid and formal versions of this, without the competitive element. Castes range from 'Untouchables' at the bottom of the social scale to Brahmins at the top, and each caste is allocated a separate social position. Despite formal secularisation, parts of India still operate a caste system, which derives from the Hindu religion. According to van den Berghe (van den Berghe, 1981, p. 164), India and South Africa are 'caste societies' in which nearly all members of a society belong to caste groups, and Japan and the United States are 'societies with caste groups'. This, however, is an unusual extension of the concept of caste.

Political scientists are generally at a loss to explain the amount and intensity of nationalist and ethnic violence in the Third World, although Horowitz is an exception. The liberal-constitutional politicians in the area are largely unable to control it, and military dictatorships often emerge. Unlike the states of the developed West, those of the Third World appear weak, and their political culture is traditional rather than modern. This means that religious and communal identities and loyalties are as important as those relating to the state. It also means that the idea of the nation is not clearly defined or accepted, so that for example Punjab national identity can refer to a territory (the Punjab, since 1947 split between India and Pakistan), a language (Punjabi), an ethnic group, or a religion (Sikh). It has been possible to build a Punjabi nationalism out of some of these identities, but impossible to build it from them all. The most virulent has been Sikh nationalism which aims to establish a Sikh state of Khalistan in or out of India. Sikh nationalism makes religion the basis of nationality. An ethnic Punjabi nation would have to include the two-thirds of Punjabis who live in Pakistan, most of whom are Moslems, not Sikhs. A language criterion for nationhood would exclude those Punjabis who speak Hindi.

While religious identity seems to have dominated Pakistani nationalism and the Khalistan national movement, language has also been the basis of nationalism in India. The linguistic states movement sought to make language the basis of the federal system, and the original states were subdivided in the 1950s in a move in this direction (in 1989 there were 25 States and 7 Union Territories in India, compared with 14 States and 6 Union Territories in 1950). Given that there are at least 1500 languages in India, this can be only a partial solution (English and Hindi are the all-Indian official languages, with 14 regional official languages). In Bangladesh, language and territory replaced religion as the national identifiers. Thus the Bengali speakers of East Pakistan split away from the Urdu speakers of West Pakistan with whom they shared a Moslem identity, and joined with Hindi speakers in Bengal to forge Bangladeshi nationalism.

What can explain the increasing salience and intensity of nationalism and ethnicity in the politics of this and other parts of Asia such as Tibet, Burma, Malaysia, the Philippines, and Fiji? (Unfortunately, there is no space to discuss all of these cases, which share features of those discussed here). And how unstable and weak is the state system which tries to cope with ethnic unrest and nationalism?

Paradoxically, it is not clear that ethnic nationalism is as important as religion or ideology across much of the continent of Asia from Lebanon to the Pacific. Indeed, nationalism seems to take second place to these in Lebanon, Afghanistan, Indochina, and China, where ethnic and linguistic conflicts seem to be relatively weak. The power of religion, and in particular of Islam, to command loyalties represents a supranational force in politics which is apparently opposed to ethnic nationalism. In Iran and Iraq, for example, Kurdish nationalism is suppressed. Moreover, the idea of nationalism and the nation-state is not as well established as that of Empire and religious community, so that national identity makes a weak basis for a state (Hugh Tinker in Tivey, 1981; Halliday and Alavi, 1988). Nevertheless, 'official nationalism' usually predominates over religion in Moslem countries, as seen in the Iran–Iraq war of the 1980s. In 1990, President Saddam Hussein of Iraq played on religion in his attempt to wage a 'Holy War' on his Arab (and Moslem) neighbours to the south. But these fellow-Arabs and Moslems were as opposed to Iraqi expansionism as non-Arabs and non-Moslems. Iraq's Pan-Arab nationalism did, however, find support in Jordan, Libya and Yemen, for reasons related to the struggle with Israel. In particular, the Palestinians saw Iraq as their principal ally.

Horowitz has argued that distinctions between 'tribal', 'linguistic' and 'religious' conflicts can no longer be usefully made in an age of pervading ethnicity (Horowitz, 1985, p. xi). For him, ethnicity dominates politics and transcends other divisions, leaving the official nationalism of the state relatively weak in many of the countries he examined (mainly in central and eastern Asia and in Africa).

It is this which explains the prevalence of ethnic conflict in these areas, and the peculiarly violent form which it takes. For the states of Asia and Africa have struggled to build nations on the basis of territories bequeathed by colonial or indigenous empires. These states are so diverse ethnically that the nation-building process has involved a massive displacement of traditional communities. Where the former empires ruled indirectly through local princes or elite groups, the new 'nation-states' seek direct authority and social homogeneity. Thus, official languages are introduced and one ethnic group often carries the 'national' identity of the state. This leaves all the other ethnic groups and languages at a disadvantage, and their reaction takes the form of ethnic nationalism. Thus in Sri Lanka the introduction of Sinhalese as the official language in the 1970s, and the consequent privileges granted to Sinhalese speakers in state employment, education, etc, provoked the Tamil nationalist reaction. The partition of Sri Lanka into two nations or federal units is the Tamil nationalist solution to the threat posed by Sinhalese nationalism.

Tamil nationalism (as Kashmiri and Punjabi nationalism) is made more complex by the international dimension. The Tamils in Sri Lanka have close ethnic ties with the Tamils in the state of Tamil Nadu in India, and these have aided the Tamil nationalists in Sri Lanka. Tamils are mainly Hindu in religion, while the Sinhalese are Buddhists. This and the language difference are the main identifiers of nationality in Sri Lanka. The Government of India has got involved, and an Indian 'peace-keeping force' was invited by the Sri Lankan government in 1987 to try to subdue the 'Tamil Tigers' terrorists, whose aim is a separate Tamil state, 'Eelam'. This operation has been only moderately successful, and resembles the interventions of the British Army in

Northern Ireland, the Syrian Army in Lebanon and the Soviet Army in Georgia and Azerbaijan. In all these cases, what is supposed to be a neutral military force is seen by many as tending to one side in the conflict. In 1989, the Sri Lankan Government asked the Indians to withdraw, but by that time they were unable to do so immediately without seeming to abandon the Tamils. For its part, the Sri Lankan Government came under attack from the Marxist Janatha Vimukhti Perumana (People's Liberation Front), a mainly Sinhalese group which engaged in terrorism in the south.

While elite cooperation between national leaders has been attempted in Sri Lanka (e.g., the abortive Bandaranaike–Chelvanayakam Pact of 1957; the Constitution of 1978 which recognised the Tamil language; the devolution proposals after 1981), its failure results from the elites' inability to control their followers. The 1957 Pact was immediately repudiated by Sinhalese militants, and the devolution proposals were attacked by these and by the Tamil Tigers. Thus one of the key conditions of consociationalism – the control by elites of their followers – is absent in Sri Lanka. By the time conciliatory moves were made to the Tamils in the late 1970s and after 1981, the extremists had become powerful. So timing in peace moves, as Horowitz has pointed out (Horowitz, 1985, pp. 577–88), is crucial. Concessions made too late may only fuel the conflict.

The intensity of conflict at the grass roots arises not only from religious and linguistic issues, but from economic ones affecting the material basis of life. The Sinhalese land colonisation policy of the 1970s invaded Tamil areas, and provoked a nationalist reaction, especially as the Tamils of the tea plantations were suffering from economic depression at that time, and were also looking for land in the same area. The policy of changing entry requirements for higher education and the awarding of quotas to ethnic groups was seen as unfair to the Tamils, as was the requirement that the Sinhala language be used as the official language. So on top of the cultural and political discontent of the Tamils, there is a strong economic motive for their nationalism as well (Arasaratnam in Boucher *et al.* (eds), 1987). This of course involves once again a cultural division of labour, which is seen in so many cases of ethnic nationalism.

The response of the Sri Lankan Government to Tamil nationalism has not been wholly negative, however. Devolution has been offered to the two Tamil Provinces in the north and east, and a kind of consociationalism is being attempted. The official use of the English language is to be encouraged, to complement the rival, and mutually hostile, Sinhala and Tamil languages.

But the Tamil Tigers wish to unite the two Tamil Provinces in one Tamil state, which would include a strong Sinhalese minority. While this is rejected by the Government, a North-Eastern Provincial Council was established in 1988 and the Eelam People's Revolutionary Liberation Front (EPRLF), which supported the pact between Sri Lanka and India (unlike the Tamil Tigers), won a majority in the election later that year. Thus a devolution alternative to the total separatism of the Tamil Tigers does exist. But the Sri Lankan government is still regarded by many Tamils as dedicated to Sinhala hegemony in a Sri Lankan 'nation-state'. Thus the existence of competing exclusive nationalisms in a political culture of violence makes accommodation between them very difficult.

It would be easy to predict the disintegration of India and Sri Lanka on account of these ethnic conflicts. But such a conclusion would be simplistic. The state of India is a complex federation of vested interests, who wish to see their local power underwritten rather than undermined (Manor, 1990). So to a lesser extent is Sri Lanka, which may well contain Tamil separatism by the devolution alternative.

As we have seen, the European ideal of the nation-state is largely foreign to Asia, with its strong tradition of empire and religious community. So some form of cultural pluralism and consociationalism within a multinational state appears to be the likely outcome, rather than a proliferation of small nation-states.

Black Africa

Nationalism in Black Africa has many features in common with that in Asia. There is a common legacy of colonialism, even more pervasive in Africa, which has practically no examples of indigenous empires or states operating independently of the European powers in the twentieth century. In terms of economic, cultural and political development, Black Africa is firmly in the 'Third World', with little industrialisation, 'high culture' or experience of liberal democracy. Here too is a political culture of violence and intercommunal conflict, with low levels of political participation and little experience of democracy. Religion has less political significance as a national identifier, except in areas in the north where Islam meets Christianity and other religions.

The first manifestation of Black African nationalism was directed against the colonial powers, and its aim was to liberate black Africans from white rule. This took the form of Pan-Africanism rather than the nationalisms of particular ethnic groups or 'nations'. Yet the struggle had to take place in the individual colonies, so that each soon produced a nationalist movement, made up largely of an educated elite, most of whom had been to Europe and had imbibed the idea of nationalism there (Arnold Hughes, in Tivey (ed.), 1981).

The reluctant withdrawal of the colonial powers from most of Africa from the late 1950s left the new rulers with the difficult task of 'nation-building' – the creation of a national community out of the mix of tribes, religions and languages which had made up the colonies. The boundaries of the colonies had been artificial lines on a map, not ethnic/social national boundaries, yet the legitimacy of the new states now rested on the consent of the people rather than on an imposed imperialism.

This was to prove impossible to obtain in several cases. Zaire (ex-Belgian Congo), Nigeria, the Sudan, and Chad all experienced long civil wars involving separatists seeking to establish their own states. The reason for these wars was not just the existence of numerous ethnic groups (tribes or 'nations' in African usage), but the fact that the new states tended to come under the control of one such group, usually numerically dominant. The resources of the state and economy were then used for the benefit of that group, to the detriment of the others. This was particularly resented by groups who possessed superior economic power, but who were denied political power, as we have seen in the European cases of the Flemings, the Catalans, and the Baltic nations.

Nigeria illustrates this too, but at the same time it points to a possible solution to the problem. In Nigeria, three dominant tribes competed for control of the new state in the 1960s. Based in the north, the numerically superior but economically inferior Moslem Hausa–Fulani tribe were able to dominate the political structure. In the west, the economically prosperous Christian Ibos sought to wrest control from the Hausas, but were repressed. They then turned to secession to form a new state, 'Biafra', which was given considerable international support. The third nation, the Yorubas in the east, were also excluded from power, but were too divided to resist.

Biafra was defeated in the Nigerian Civil War (1967–70), but the result was not a revival of Hausa–Fulani domination. Successive

Constitutions were adopted, the last being in 1979, in elaborate attempts to satisfy tribal and regional interests, while continuing to build a Nigerian nation. Although the most recent civilian rule lasted only from 1979 to 1983, the military government of Nigeria has retained some of the features of the 1979 Constitution under a new draft Constitution (1989), and promises to restore civilian rule entirely in 1992.

The new Nigerian Constitution imposes a 'national ethic' with a national motto, national anthem and coat of arms. There is a constitutional obligation to 'actively encourage national integration' so that 'loyalty to the nation shall override sectional loyalties'. However, 'the state shall foster a feeling of belonging and involvement among the various peoples of the Federation'. This is partly reflected in the existence of 21 states in the Federation, although these do not correspond to nations (tribes/'peoples'). The Government of the Federation must ensure that there shall be 'no predominance of persons from a few states or from a few ethnic or other sectional groups'. This means that a quota system operates, giving shares of government employment to the citizens of each state. The Cabinet must contain one 'indigene' from each state, and the army must 'reflect the federal character of Nigeria'. The President is to be elected by at least a quarter of the votes cast in each of at least two-thirds of all the states. At the same time, ethnic emblems and labels are banned for federal political parties, which are virtually established by the federal government. In the 21 states, preference is given to 'indigenes' in public employment.

Nigeria has thus attempted to produce a form of consociationalism on the basis of a rather arbitrary division of the country into 21 states. These states are not nations or even tribes, although there is usually a dominant tribe in each state. Thus the challenge of ethnic nationalism remains. It may be that in the long run, tribal and ethnic divisions can be altered and even eliminated, leaving one Nigerian social nation. Crawford Young has shown that many tribes in Africa were in fact the artificial creation of the colonial regimes (Crawford Young, 1976, pp. 34–7), and so it may be possible to create 'peoples' in Nigeria to conform with the federal structure. Alternatively, it may be possible to neutralise them politically by superimposing a constitutional structure which cuts across them. In place of ethnic loyalties there would be regional and political loyalties based on local power units. But success in this, as we have seen from other cases of nationalism, depends on satisfying a wide range of political, cultural and economic demands.

South Africa and Apartheid

South Africa, like Quebec, was a colony settled by two distinct European states, the Netherlands and Britain. Its 'colonial nationalism' was thus similarly divided ethnically, which led to constant conflicts between the settlers of Dutch origin (known as Afrikaners or Boers) and the British, culminating in the 'Boer War' of 1899–1902. A reconciliation on the basis of one white South African colonial 'official' nation was achieved in 1910, when a largely independent Union of South Africa was established. This nation was not an 'ethnic' or 'social' nation, however, since the Afrikaners and British retained their own languages, churches, and intermarriage patterns. The 'official' national basis of the Union of South Africa excluded the native (black) and immigrant Asian (coloured) population, whose position was that of subjugation, both economically and politically (Eddy and Schreuder, 1988). It is obvious that an internal colonialist explanation fits this situation very well, since one cultural ('racial') group (albeit ethnically divided) exploited the others (see Greenberg, 1980).

A regime change occurred in 1948. In that year, the Afrikaner-based National Party won the elections, and proceeded to institute its policy of apartheid or 'separate development' of the races. This involved a more rigorous racial segregation between blacks and whites, especially with regard to land settlement and housing. The races are divided (1985 estimate) into Whites (18%), Africans (68%), Coloureds (10%) and Asians (3%), each of which is legally identified and given special treatment. Under Afrikaner National Party rule, the residue of white colonial nationalism represented by the British settlers became largely ineffective. Although apartheid was the Afrikaner National Party policy, the whites as a whole supported the main practices of racial segregation. A few were leading opponents, and these were usually of British origin.

Black nationalism is mainly represented by the African National Congress (ANC), although that organisation is open to all irrespective of colour. It was founded as far back as 1912, in reaction to the 1910 Union settlement, but its main impact was to come in the period after 1948. In 1960, under National Party rule, it was outlawed, and black rebellions such as those of 1960 and 1976 were brutally repressed. Deprived of constitutional status and electoral opportunities in South Africa, the ANC had its headquarters in Zambia, which supported its aims while keeping up international relations with South Africa. In

February 1990 it was legalised, and many of its leaders released from prison, including Nelson Mandela.

Apartheid arouses intense international interest, mostly hostile. Pressure from abroad, including limited economic sanctions, is perhaps as important as internal activities in shaping nationalist politics in South Africa. The economic prosperity of the whites is threatened by the international attacks on the apartheid regime, and changing economic interests affecting commerce, mining and farming have led to the National Party's change of policy in the 1980s, whereby apartheid is ostensibly to be gradually dismantled. The main losers in this process are the whites whose position was protected by an all-white policy of employment in the public services.

The result is that splits have occurred on both sides of the racial divide. On the white side, 16 right-wing MPs of the National Party defected in 1982 to form the Conservative Party, which became the official opposition after the 1987 elections, with increased representation in the 1989 elections. The Conservatives object to any fundamental reform of the apartheid system. On the extreme right, there is a neo-fascist Afrikaner Resistance Movement. Within the National Party itself, the new official policy of dismantling apartheid is challenged by the old guard, but others who support majority rule (or power-sharing with blacks) split off in 1989 to form the Democratic Party, which replaced the Progressive Federal Party as the political voice of liberal whites. It increased its representation in 1989, but remained a minor party. Thus the National Party was squeezed electorally from both the conservative and liberal sides. Yet it still retained its majority position.

On the non-white side, the ANC, though the dominant black nationalist organisation, long had to face the fact that it was an illegal organisation in South Africa. Other black organisations, such as the United Democratic Front and the Azanian People's Organisation (AZAPO), have operated under emergency restrictions since 1988. In 1989 the Mass Democratic Movement was formed as a surrogate for the ANC to lead the black attack on apartheid. Black nationalists are to some extent split in their aims between the ANC position of espousing majority rule based on all citizens and the AZAPO and Pan-Africanist Congress position of explicitly seeking a black nation in which non-blacks would have to apply for citizenship. While both strategies would produce black rule in practice, the latter is clearly more in line with 'ethnic nationalism', the former with 'social nationalism'.

Black nationalism is further complicated by the politics of Chief

Mangosutho Buthelezi's Zulu-based Inkatha movement, which has supported a form of power-sharing with the white regime on the basis of the tribal homelands. There are complex feuds in the black townships, which some describe as tribal in nature, but which can also be seen as relating to divergent economic and political interests. Buthelezi has declared in favour of majority rule for South Africa, but the intense rivalry between his supporters and those of the ANC has led to considerable death and injury, which has increased since the ANC was legalised in 1990. Buthelezi is seen by the ANC as the pawn of the white regime, and his Zulu Police have attacked ANC supporters with the protection of the South African Police. Here the issue seems to be local power and patronage: the Inkatha is threatened by the ANC and turns to the white Government for protection. Both factions in the black community have resorted to violence and operate outside constitutional methods.

In addition, the Indians have their own nationalist organisations, though the 'Coloureds' (mixed race) have been forced by the Group Areas Act, which determines where they can live, and by their limited role in the government, to identify with black nationalism. This is despite the 1984 Constitutional change in which the Coloureds were one of the three groups (the others were Whites and Indians) to be granted an elected chamber each in the South African legislature.

The existence of several distinct national and racial communities in South Africa makes consociationalism (power-sharing) an attractive form of government as a democratic alternative to apartheid or to simple majority rule (Lijphart, 1985). The white Progressive Federal Party (now defunct) and the black Inkatha movement of Natal espoused something like this. F. W. de Clerk's Nationalist Government in 1989 announced a five-year plan to dismantle apartheid based on racial groups in favour of a kind of consociationalism based on 'cultural groups', all of which would be equal participants in the political process. What difference this would make to the practice of apartheid is not clear, especially as informal segregation in education and housing would likely remain. The ANC rejects consociationalism because it denies majority rule and is based on group rights rather than individual rights. Black ethnic nationalists reject it because it explicitly denies the idea of South Africa as a black nation. Similarly, right-wing white nationalists are opposed, since to them it threatens to destroy white domination.

The conditions for the successful introduction of consociational democracy will be discussed in Chapter 9. Here it can be said that the partial dismantling of apartheid since the late 1980s as a result of internal and external economic and political pressures gives hope that some of these conditions might be met. But other necessary conditions are absent, the most important being that there should be cooperation between the groups on the basis of equality. This is still a long way off in South Africa as far as most whites are concerned. Moreover, black and white nationalisms fight each other for exclusive control of the same territory, which each calls its own. In a consociational system, territorial claims are usually met by partition, but that solution in the form of 'black homelands' has already failed to satisfy black nationalists. Should apartheid be abolished and a consociational system established, this would still leave open the likelihood that a cultural division of labour would continue, albeit on a less formal basis. An ethnic-class domination by whites might replace the constitutional domination which they exercise in the system of apartheid.

Zionism and Palestinian Nationalism

A similar struggle for territory takes place in the Middle East, in the area known in history as Palestine. A distinctive form of nationalist ideology, Zionism, was developed in the late 19th century by Theodor Herzl in *The Jewish State* (1896) in which Palestine was claimed as the 'national home for the Jewish people'. This was accepted by the British Government in the Balfour Declaration of 1917, for reasons which remain rather obscure. After a period of increased Jewish settlement in Palestine under the British-administered League of Nations Mandate, the state of Israel was unilaterally declared by Zionist militants in 1948.

An opposing nationalism, that of the Palestinians, had arisen in reaction to Zionism. Most of these were refugees in neighbouring Arab states, but some remained as second-class citizens in Israel. The Palestinians contest Israel's claim to its present territory, although since 1989 Palestinian nationalism as represented by the Palestine Liberation Organisation (PLO) has conceded the right of the state of Israel to exist in some form. The PLO, however, like the ANC in South Africa from 1960 to 1990, is proscribed in Israel.

Considerable conflict exists in the Israeli settlements which have extended the 1948 borders of Israel to the West bank of the River Jordan and to the Gaza strip. Since December 1987, an 'Uprising' (*intifada*) of Palestinian Arabs in the Gaza Strip under the auspices of organisations such as the Unified National Leadership for the Uprising has dominated the politics of Palestine. Meanwhile, the Israeli political system has been marked by instability and the need to satisfy extremist Zionist parties. This has been the result of the proportional representation electoral system which has made Israeli Governments dependent on small parties of an extreme nationalist and religious character. These political pressures have led to the extension of Jewish settlements in Palestinian areas and to heightened conflicts between Jews and Arabs.

All this seems to amount to a clash of apparently irreconcilable nationalisms. Both Palestinians and Jews claim that Palestine is their homeland, and neither is prepared to concede the other's claim, although some sort of *modus vivendi* is clearly required. Once again, a form of consociationalism might be appropriate, allowing for Palestinian self-government in the Israeli state. But since the conflict is essentially about national control over the same territory, consociationalism, which is usually based on communities with separate territories in the same state, may not be possible as long as these claims persist.

Conflicting nationalisms of this kind are not unusual. As we have seen, Irish nationalists (and the Constitution of the Republic of Ireland) and Unionists both claim Northern Ireland for their nation, and the territory of South Africa is claimed for the Afrikaner nation and for the black African nation. But Zionism adds an extra dimension to Israeli nationalism which makes it more of an ethnic nationalism than a social nationalism. Although Zionism is a comparatively recent form of nationalist ideology (the first Zionist Congress met in Switzerland in 1897), its basis is to be found in the long and tortuous history of the Jewish nation, which is perhaps the oldest in continuous existence. The elements of this history – the forced dispersal of the Jewish nation from Palestine (the diaspora); the persecutions and anti-Semitism culminating in the Nazi holocaust; the comparatively recent settlement of Jews in Palestine as a result of the Balfour Declaration of 1917; the turbulent circumstances of the establishment of the state of Israel in 1948, leading to constant warfare with its Arab neighbours and to opposition from its own Arab population – are not reproduced in any other case, and make Israeli national identity and nationalism perhaps the strongest in world history.

But only one part of Jewish nationalism is represented by Zionism. Most Jews prefer to be citizens of states other than Israel and to have dual national identity (Jewish, and that of the state they live in). Zionism is often embarrassing to them because it implies that Israel is the only rightful national home for Jews. While rejecting this, many non-Zionist Jews support Israel in international affairs, and the Jewish lobby in the United States is extremely successful in influencing the US government to maintain its massive aid to Israel (see Chapter 10).

Israel may be a settler nation, as Protestant Northern Ireland, French Quebec, and white South Africa, but the Jewish settlers, unlike these settlers, claim that they have 'come home'. There is thus an extra emotional dimension to Zionism which is not found in colonial settler nationalisms (see Teodor Shanin, 'The Zionisms of Israel' in Halliday and Alavi, 1988). Israel is an ethnic nation rather than a social nation, in that it is explicitly the nation of the Jews, and cannot in theory become a nation in which Jews are a minority. Under the Law of Return, all Jews have the right to live there, and although all citizens are guaranteed equality of social and political rights, non-Jews cannot serve in the army. It is thus a particularly intractable form of nationalism with regard to the members of ethnic minorities in the state, who must be considered to some extent second-class citizens, and certainly irrelevant to the *rationale* of the state.

Even within the Jewish people, there is controversy over the question 'Who is a Jew?' The Law of Return uses an ethnic definition (descent from a Jewish mother), but Orthodox Jews prefer religious credentials, which could include conversion to Orthodox Judaism of non-Jews. The declaration of the State of Israel in 1948 proclaimed 'the natural right of the Jewish people to be master of its own fate, like all other nations, in its own sovereign state', and it said that Israel would 'be open for Jewish immigration and for the ingathering of exiles'. These Jews came from widely differing backgrounds, including a variety of languages and even skin colours. This made the Jewish nation in Israel a most complex entity, socially and politically, with strong pressure to produce a 'social nation' or cultural homogeneity out of what was apparently (but not really) a homogeneous Jewish ethnicity.

Even without cultural homogeneity, the Israelis are united behind one of the strongest nationalisms in the world. That is because internal differences largely disappear when faced with the external threat to the Israeli state. A series of wars with its Arab neighbours from the foundation of the state has greatly heightened Israeli nationalism, so that it is as much a function of international relations as of Zionist ideology. This will be discussed further in the chapter on Nationalism in International Relations (Chapter 10).

Conclusion to Case-studies

The wide variety of case-studies presented in this book makes it difficult to provide a simple conclusion about nationalist movements and ethnic politics (a more general theoretical conclusion on the politics of nationalism and ethnicity will be given in Chapter 11). From Sri Lanka to Quebec, and from Scotland to South Africa, nationalists differ from each other as much as these countries differ.

Some nationalists aim at 'autonomy' for their nation, others at complete independence. Some use the methods of the ballot box, others resort to violence, even genocide. Some are highly educated and middle-class, others ill-educated and poor. Nationalist parties are occasionally strong electorally, but mostly they are weak, perhaps because there are several in competition with each other. Nationalist political behaviour outside nationalist parties is much more widespread, sometimes encompassing nearly all the nation. Only a study of each case can reveal the reasons for these differences, but there are features in common. One is the conjunction of ethnic and economic divisions, encapsulated in the model of the cultural division of labour. That situation leads to nationalism, which is heightened if 'internal colonialism' is also present.

Another common feature is the presence of a 'regime change' in a state, which releases nationalism by providing the opportunity for nationalist political action. Without this, nationalism is latent, static, or repressed. The USSR, Spain, Yugoslavia, and Quebec provide examples of sudden regime changes leading to the equally sudden emergence of strong nationalist movements.

Of course, the wider context of social and economic change is part of the explanation for regime change. Serious economic decline (USSR, Yugoslavia), or sudden economic resurgence (Catalonia, Quebec, Scotland), often accompany regime changes. More particularly, economic and social changes which adversely affect particular nations and ethnic groups in their relationship with others leads to nationalism. Thus opposition to immigrant labour, to 'foreign' economic control, or to industrialisation, and to environmental pollution, have been rallying calls of nationalist movements in the Soviet Baltic nations and in the Basque country.

Nationalist movements vary considerably in the amount and character of the support they command. Separatists are rarely supported by a majority of the nation, unless there is a background of strong oppression, or a recent history of independent statehood (e.g., the Baltic states were independent until 1940). Most nationalists are prepared to settle for autonomy, and some are only cultural nationalists with no desire for political institutions. Finally, there are unionists or loyalists in the nation who support the status quo, or even further centralisation. Fitting people into these different categories is not easy, but it can be said that those with something to gain economically from a particular political system will likely support it. Thus big business and central government elites (including their agents in the nation) are likely to oppose sub-state nationalism, while national cultural elites and small business people will tend to be nationalist. This leaves the mass of the people open to persuasion by either side. For them, a perception of political oppression and economic deprivation is crucial if they are to become actively nationalist. The credibility and efficiency of nationalist leaders will be important in making up the people's minds, and the degree of openness of the political system will determine the 'capability factor' for nationalist political behaviour. In conditions of repression, not many will seek to become martyrs.

Ethnic politics differs from nationalism in that it does not have as its rationale 'national self-determination' in a territorial homeland. Instead the aim is the maximum advantage for the ethnic group within a multiethnic state. Ethnic groups may see themselves as part of a wider nation, such as the 'American nation' or the 'British nation', or they may see themselves as separate nations (Black nationalists in the US, and tribal 'nationalists' in African states). Even if the latter, their nationalism may not amount to separatism.

The demands of nationalists vary. At one end of the spectrum, complete independence for the nation through separation may be the aim. This is the classical nationalist prescription. At the other end, official nationalists whose loyalty is to the state follow a 'nation-building' strategy through which different nations and ethnic groups are assimilated or integrated into a new, homogeneous state. This is the nationalism of immigrant nations such as the US, and of the new successor states of the European colonial empires.

If neither of these is acceptable or appropriate, the answer must be a form of political accommodation or 'consociationalism' in which the nations or ethnic groups live together in one state on the basis of an equal partnership. In such a state, each nation can achieve a limited national self-determination but not a separate nation-state. Since most states fight fiercely to prevent secessions, political accommodation and the consociational model are more attractive to moderate nationalists than the classical nation-state model. It is also an answer to the threat which 'majority rule' systems pose to permanent minorities such as the Roman Catholics in Northern Ireland and the whites in South Africa. The features and conditions of political accommodation in a multinational state form the subject of the next chapter.

9

Cultural Pluralism and the Politics of Accommodation

Most states in the world are multinational and multiethnic. Thus the classical nationalist ideal of 'one nation, one state' can only be achieved by a process of nation-building to assimilate all citizens into one nation, or by domination or expulsion of the citizens who do not belong to the nation, viewed as an historic ethnic community. This is the aim of *integral* or *exclusive* nationalism, and its effects have been unfortunate in those states whose social basis is multiethnic or multicultural. Such nationalism is highly intolerant of national minorities and in history it has been linked with Fascism and Nazism, and with those states which have repressed or expelled the national minorities within them (for 'integral nationalism', see Alter, 1989, pp. 37–54).

These nationalists have shown the extreme version of nationalism, and have alienated many commentators from nationalism altogether (Kedourie, 1960; Minogue, 1967; Birch, 1989; Hobsbawm, 1990). Yet it is possible to see other forms of nationalism in a more positive light, and to find nationalism which does not stick at the classical formulation of national homogeneity within one state. This nationalism accepts that a stable and free society can be based on cultural pluralism, in a multinational state based on political accommodation and democracy.

Consociational Democracy

Political scientists since the late 1960s have been very active studying how such a state can be established (Lijphart, 1968, 1977, 1984, 1985; Young, 1976; Horowitz, 1985). Lijphart invented the phrase 'consociational democracy' (otherwise known as 'consociationalism' and, in a later less rigid version, 'consensus democracy'), to describe a special form of democracy devised to cope with the problems of extreme

135

'cultural pluralism' (otherwise known as 'segmented pluralism', 'segmented societies', or 'divided societies'). In the context of the politics of nationalism and ethnicity it provides a model of government which allows for the peaceful coexistence of more than one nation or ethnic group in the state on the basis of separation, yet equal partnership rather than the domination by one nation of the other(s). It is thus not only an alternative to the principle of 'one nation, one state', but also to systems of 'hegemony', and 'internal colonialism'.

Lijphart first used the term 'consociational democracy' to describe the political system of the Netherlands (Lijphart, 1968), which, while democratic, did not at the time of writing follow the pattern of majoritarian systems such as those of Britain, France, and Italy. Rather, it was based on a complex system of political representation and safeguards for the five social segments or 'pillars' (*verzuiling*) of Dutch society: one Catholic, two Protestant, one Socialist, and one Liberal. These 'pillars' formed a system of 'cultural pluralism' consisting of largely self-contained, isolated 'societies'. Each society had its own political party, trade unions, schools, newspapers, and time on radio and television. Marriages across the societies were rare, and citizens did not often even make friends across them.

It is easy to find examples of divided societies in many parts of the world, although they are not all exactly like the Netherlands as described by Lijphart (and the Netherlands has changed since the 1960s). They include Northern Ireland (Catholics and Protestants); Lebanon (Christians and Moslems); Sri Lanka (Tamils and Sinhalese); Malaysia (Malays and Chinese); Canada (Francophones and Anglophones); and South Africa (Blacks, Whites and 'Coloureds' in the old apartheid system). All these have attempted, or are attempting, some form of the consociational system.

Lijphart's description of the system in the Netherlands led him to examine what seemed to be similar consociational democracies in Europe (Belgium, Switzerland, and Austria) and elsewhere (e.g., Lebanon, Malaysia, and Canada) (Lijphart, 1977). Later, he considered whether consociationalism could be a solution to the problems of deeply divided societies such as Northern Ireland and South Africa, where majority rule was unacceptable to the minority (Lijphart, 1985). There is thus both a descriptive and prescriptive side to writings on consociational democracy (see also McRae, 1974; van den Berghe, 1981; and Horowitz, 1985).

These and other political scientists and sociologists have followed

Lijphart's lead in defining consociationalism, and it is now possible to look at the model in terms of the politics of nationalism and ethnicity generally to see what its features are and what conditions are conducive to its success. 'Consociational democracy', as presented by Lijphart, is an 'ideal form' of political accommodation in multinational states, and in the real world there are many variations of it, and some other forms of political accommodation which will be discussed later.

In this ideal consociational democracy, the following institutional arrangements are found:

(1) A 'Grand Coalition' in the government of the state, consisting of representatives of all the segments (for our purposes, 'nations' or 'ethnic groups'). This is otherwise known as 'elite accommodation', since it is the leaders ('elites') of the segments who come together at the centre of the state to settle disputes.
(2) A proportional representation electoral system, and a proportional system for sharing public expenditure and public employment amongst the segments according to the size of each.
(3) A 'mutual veto' system, whereby a segment can veto government decisions in matters of vital concern to it.
(4) Autonomy for each segment, either through a territorial government in a federal or devolution system, or through institutions (e.g., educational) which confer some self-government on the segment.

These are the institutional features which typically characterise an ideal consociational system. Such systems (with all or most of the features present) have operated in 'divided societies' – some divided along the lines of nationality and ethnicity, and others along ideological and religious lines, or some combination of the two. We are concerned with the former, and the principal examples are Belgium, Switzerland, Canada, Nigeria, Northern Ireland during 'power-sharing', and for a short time Sri Lanka and Malaysia. Multinational states which have some, but not all, consociational features are the USSR, Yugoslavia, Spain, and the UK. In these states, federal, quasi-federal, devolved, or decentralised systems exist which recognise the multinational character of the states. The rights of the several nations are enshrined in the constitution and are balanced against those of the overall majority or of the largest segment. Unlike consociationalism however, the political systems in such states give the majority final authority in a conflict between it and a segment (in communist systems, the majority is usually represented by the state-wide Communist Party).

Despite some successes, the history of consociationalism has been marked by tensions and breakdown. Belgium has continuing strife (mostly non-violent) between Flemings and Walloons; Switzerland had a civil war in the 19th century and a separatist movement in the Jura in the 1970s; in Northern Ireland power-sharing collapsed in 1974 after a brief existence; in Lebanon, Nigeria, Sri Lanka and Malaysia there are only echoes of consociationalism while civil wars rage or have just recently ceased. Of the consociational countries still operating as such, perhaps only Switzerland is entirely politically stable today. Yet the consociational system remains probably the best (ideal) way to combine several nations in one state on the basis of partnership rather than domination.

What are the favourable conditions for consociational democracy? Liphart gave seven structural factors which he felt were conducive to the success of consociationalism (Lijphart, 1977), although he also stressed the importance of 'a creative and constructive act of free will' by elites, whose qualities could overcome any deficiencies in these factors (Lijphart, 1968, p. 195).

The seven favourable conditions, according to Lijphart, are:

(1) A multiple balance of power among the segments rather than a dual balance of power or the hegemony of one of the segments.
(2) Small rather than large countries.
(3) The power of elites to get the acceptance of their followers to the process of 'elite accommodation'.
(4) Homogeneous and isolated segments rather than internally divided and scattered segments.
(5) The existence of overarching loyalties to the state beyond those to the segments.
(6) A tradition of accommodation prior to the coming of mass democracy.
(7) The existence of cross-cutting divisions (eg, class, religion, language) across the segments.

Pappalardo, in his critique of Lijphart's 'conditions' (Pappalardo, 1981), points to evidence which suggests that not all of these conditions are necessary or even conducive to the success of consociational democracy. After examining again the examples used by Lijphart, he concludes that 'Only two conditions are unambiguously favourable to consociational cooperation: inter-subcultural stability and elite predominance over a politically deferential and organizationally encap-sulated following' (*ibid.*, p. 365). Put more simply, consociationalism is most likely to work if the segments (nations or ethnic groups) do not change in size or in importance relatively to one another. Examples of such threatened groups are the Christians in Lebanon and the Protestants in Northern Ireland. The former are increasingly outnumbered by the Moslems, and the latter 'outbred' by the Catholics. Such changes may induce one of them to break free from the pattern of accommodation to aim for dominance, and make a declining segment feel it is losing out in the system, so that it too ceases to cooperate. The second condition refers to the ability of the segments' leaders to control the rank-and-file. Without this control, the 'accommodation' between the elites is in vain. Instead, revolts and extremism take its place at the grass-roots and the system collapses. Thus in 1974, the 'power-sharing' Executive set up by Protestant and Catholic leaders was brought down by a combination of a Protestant Workers' strike and IRA violence.

We have already seen in some of the case-studies in Chapters 6, 7, and 8 examples of countries which have attempted to operate consociational systems, and the difficulties they have experienced. We can now relate these difficulties to the presence or absence of the seven 'conditions' listed above.

Perhaps the most important favourable condition is the first: the presence of more than two segments, with no one segment in a majority position. In a state made up of two nations or ethnic groups, the temptation is always present for the larger to seek to promote a 'nation-state' through exclusion or assimilation of the smaller. This is not as likely in a multinational state in which there is no dominant nation. Bicommunal societies such as Northern Ireland, Sri Lanka, Malaysia, and Fiji have failed to produce consociationalism, since the majority community has sought and achieved domination (in the case of Fiji, the Fijians are actually a smaller group than the Indians, but retained control of the state by a military coup in 1987 after an election was won by an Indian-dominated coalition).

In contrast to these failures, bipolar consociationalism has had some success in Canada where, as we have seen, the rights of francophones and anglophones are protected in the Constitution, with Quebec gen-erally recognised as a 'distinct society' within Canada. Indeed, the only other ethnic group of importance, the Indians, have largely lost out in this settlement. In Belgium, the division is largely between the

Dutch and French speakers, who together make up over 90% of the population (there are also small German and Frisian populations). The Flemish (Dutch-speaking) group is the clear majority (c. 60%), but a consociational system has been established which is quite successful (it covers the German community as well). The government of the capital, Brussels, is made up of representatives from both communities, and there is a French-speaking majority. The condition of autonomy for each segment is impossible on a territorial basis in Brussels, since the populations are living together, though there is some residential segregation. Instead a system of 'personal' autonomy is operating, with separate schools for members of each community under a common Brussels authority which neither community entirely controls.

The conditions which have been favourable in Belgium include a tradition of consociationalism (the previous system was based on religion, not language), and overarching loyalty to the state (few Flemings wish to join the Netherlands, or Walloons to join France). Autonomy for the communities has been introduced in stages, and there is now in effect a federal system based on the territorial segregation of the language communities, except for Brussels. The smallness of the country may be favourable, though Pappalardo rejects this condition, since there are examples of large countries such as Canada and the USSR which operate moderately successfully on consociational principles, and small countries (Northern Ireland, Sri Lanka, Fiji) failing to do so.

The failures of consociationalism derive from internal and external forces which prevent 'elite accommodation'. Clearly, the inability of the leadership to control the followers makes the whole system difficult, if not impossible, to sustain. Moderate nationalists (e.g., the Social and Democratic Labour Party in Northern Ireland) may be faced with the opposition of more extreme nationalists (the IRA and Sinn Fein) and the segment fragments. Similar fragmentations have occurred in most nationalist movements, but it may still be possible to preserve the authority of the leadership. Thus the moderate Catalan nationalists and the Liberals in Quebec speak effectively for their nations. The moderate Tamil and Sinhalese leaderships, however, are faced with civil war in their attempt to introduce consociationalism in Sri Lanka.

The cases of Northern Ireland and Sri Lanka point up another major problem for consociational democracy – the presence of outside loyalties and interference. The nationalists in Northern Ireland regard Ireland as their nation, and have no loyalty to a separate Northern Ireland. Outside support from the Republic of Ireland, and from Irish descendants in the US, has sustained the the IRA and Sinn Fein, while on the Unionist side, the British state has helped defend the Union, even if it has also tried to promote power-sharing.

The Tamil nationalists in India have received help from India, and the Indian Army was invited in to keep the peace in the Tamil areas in 1987. The collapse of consociationalism in the Lebanon since 1974 is largely explainable in terms of outside interference in the affairs of Lebanon by Israel, Syria, Iran, and Iraq, each of which has its client groups in the country. The internal shift in the balance of power between the segments has also contributed to the collapse of the 1943–75 system of consociationalism. The Moslems have grown in number in comparison with the Christians, so that they now form a majority of the population, but the latter are unwilling to change the complex constitutional rules which share power between the communities. As an exception to the general rule about the negative character of outside interference, it was a combination of Arab nations (the Arab League) which tried to restore consociationalism in Lebanon in 1989, but this did not gain the support of a section of the grassroots Christians, since they were to be deprived of their dominant position. So by seeking different versions of consociationalism, the external and internal forces have prevented it being re-established in the Lebanon.

Lijphart has suggested that consociational democracy might be a solution to the communal problems of South Africa (Lijphart, 1985). As we have seen in Chapter 8, the National Party, and to some extent the Democratic Party, have proposed something along the lines of consociationalism: a form of democracy which, while involving all citizens, preserves 'cultural' identities and rights. To Black nationalists in the ANC and Pan-Africanist Congress this represents apartheid under another name, but for Lijphart and the Democrats it is in line with the liberal traditions of European consociational democracy. The Zulu Inkatha movement is also more favourable to consociationalism, as such a system might protect its rights against the ANC and majority rule. Moreover, as we have seen, there are black African states with features of consociationalism, notably Nigeria.

But are the 'conditions' for consociational democracy present in South Africa? In their critique of Lijphart, McGarry and Noel (1989) conclude that although these conditions are not present today, since the whites apparently aim at domination not real power-sharing, 'consociational democracy nevertheless remains the only form of democracy with any prospect whatsoever of being more or less peacefully attained' (*ibid.*, p. 19). They also say that 'a continuation of non-democratic rule and worsening violence is the likeliest prospect'.

Black nationalists of the ANC seek majority rule with no 'group rights', but they may be forced to reconsider this if the alternative is prolonged civil war, between tribes such as the Zulus and the Xhosas. The whites, for their part, are likely to move towards a version of consociationalism in their dismantling of apartheid. Perhaps in this case Lijphart's optimism is misplaced, but there have been cases of fundamental shifts in interethnic relations towards cooperation where before there was conflict, such as Switzerland, Belgium, Austria and the Netherlands. These have come from the realisation of the groups themselves that conflict was unprofitable, or from external force imposing a new system. The unwillingness of the international community to intervene decisively in South Africa on the side of the democratic forces means that only an internal settlement can produce consociationalism. For this, new elites are required with supportive followers to enter into an 'accommodation'. The alternatives are domination or civil war. It is in this light that consociationalism can appear an attractive alternative to exclusive nationalism in a culturally plural society.

Other Forms of Political Accommodation

Horowitz, in his *Ethnic Groups in Conflict* (Horowitz, 1985), while seeking a political system which reduces ethnic conflict, finds fault with consociationalism on the grounds that it makes *a priori* assumptions about the effects of constitutional arrangements on ethnic conflict. In the real world, he says, things are not that simple. In particular, Asian and African countries differ from the European consociational democracies in many ways, particularly in the strength of their 'ascriptive' characteristics, such as appearance, language, religion, and so on. According to him, to solidify these in separate constitutional segments is a dangerous strategy. He is thus critical of the assumption that the maintenance of homogeneous ethnic segments makes accommodation between them easier. Rather, he sees multiethnic political units as more cooperative with one another. In any case, homogeneous segments (nations or ethnic groups) are not common in Third World countries, or indeed anywhere, for each segment is split into rival factions or parties. Thus a 'Grand Coalition' of the leaders of the ethnic groups in a state is likely to be challenged by splinter groups.

In place of a uniform pattern of consociational devices, Horowitz provides a set of constitutional solutions appropriate to different situations of ethnic conflict. While some of these are the same as in consociational democracy, others are not. There is the same emphasis on proportional representation in the electoral system and of proportionality of rewards between ethnic groups. But he is suspicious of 'preferential' schemes which benefit one group – even a 'backward' group – disproportionately. This can lead to a backlash among groups who are discriminated against under such 'affirmative action' policies.

Autonomy through federalism or devolution is supported, but not necessarily on the basis of giving each ethnic group its own state. Rather, the aim is to break down ethnic cohesion by inducing inter-ethnic cooperation and intraethnic competition. This can be done by increasing the number of federal units, as in Nigeria and India, to prevent the nations (ethnic groups) corresponding exactly with the states of the federation, which, according to him, would be a recipe for ethnic conflict unless the ethnic groups are internally subdivided and likely to compete within the state (federal unit). Unlike the consociationalists, he considers that a presidential system (as in Nigeria, Sri Lanka, and Malaysia) can work as well as a Grand Coalition, if accompanied by an electoral system which ensures that several ethnic groups must participate in the presidential majority vote. He rejects partition ('not the policy of choice but of desperation' (p. 592)) and international regional integration, as in the ill-fated Federation of Malaysia in 1963, covering Malaysia, Sarawak, Sabah and Singapore ('it seems inevitably to favor one or another of the contestants' (p. 595)).

Instead, he suggests 'Five mechanisms of conflict reduction' (*ibid.*, pp. 597–600):

(1) proliferating the points of power so as to take the heat off a single focal point (e.g., 'separation of powers' between branches of government at the centre and division of powers between the central government and regional governments);

(2) arrangements which emphasise intraethnic conflict rather than interethnic conflict (e.g., competition for reserved offices for members of an ethnic group, and territorial devolution, giving rise to party competition within the nation);

(3) policies that create incentives for interethnic cooperation (e.g., electoral inducements for coalition);

(4) policies that encourage alignments based on interests other than

ethnicity;

(5) reducing disparities between groups so that dissatisfaction declines.

Some of these are policy measures rather than institutional arrangements. Unlike consociationalism, most of Horowitz's prescriptions aim
to break down or divide ethnic segments rather than to maintain them.
Even so, they do not seek to eradicate ethnic differences through
'nation-building', but to provide incentives for ethnic groups to live
peaceably together. While some may appear to be mutually contradictory in practice (e.g., (4) and (5), since preferential or 'affirmative
action' policies emphasise group identities rather than cross-group
interests), they do represent a useful agenda for policy-makers trying
to solve the problems of ethnic and national conflict. As Horowitz says
(p. 600), 'Ethnic problems are intractable, but they are not altogether
without hope'. He sums up his preferred aims of policy with regard
to ethnic groups as '*fragmentation, moderation, coalition, fluidity* and
proportionality' (p. 646).

Horowitz concludes that failures to deal with ethnic conflict do
not derive from a lack of knowledge as to what to do, or from
'an unalterable human nature', but from deficiencies in political will
(p. 684). This 'enlightenment'-style rationalism, however, and that of
the consociationalists generally, presupposes that nationalist and ethnocentric behaviour is responsive to constitutional manipulation and that
a 'rational' 'cost-benefit analysis' will be adopted by all those involved
(for a similar 'Rational Choice' approach to nationalist politics see
Tiryakian and Rogowski, 1985, chapters 4–6).

The seemingly irrational, instinctive, and emotional side to nationalist behaviour makes it difficult, perhaps impossible, for political
engineering to produce predictable results. As can be seen from Horowitz's own extensive array of examples, very few of the methods
he prescribes have worked for long, as other factors have become
more important than the constitutional arrangements. Consociational
arrangements collapsed in Lebanon, Cyprus, Nigeria, and Sri Lanka,
and are fragile in Belgium, Canada and Malaysia. They seem to have
been replaced by competitive democracy in the Netherlands. Thus,
the scope for altering nationalist political behaviour by constitutional
reform is limited, for that behaviour is determined by a wide range of
influences, from the instinctive to the party political, in a context of
(non-constitutional) cultural and economic change. To control all these
together is so far beyond the skills of political science. Nevertheless,

consociationalism and other mechanisms for conflict reduction are probably the best political tools available to produce peace in 'divided societies'. As the present state system is a rigid one which opposes the secession of nations from multinational states, the consociational model and its variants give such nations some hope of satisfying their nationalisms without resorting to civil war.

10

Nationalism and International Relations

The critical importance of nationalism in international relations is recognised in the received wisdom that 'nationalism' caused both World Wars in the 20th century. Much of international history since 1800 has been concerned with nationalism, and in Europe alone it forced the break-up of the multinational Russian, Austrian, and Ottoman Empires, the separation of Norway from Sweden and of Ireland from Britain. Also in Europe, nationalism unified Italy and Germany, so that each formed a 'nation-state', even if many Germans still lived outside Germany. After 1945, nationalism greatly increased the number of states in the world when the colonised peoples of the European empires in the Third World fought their way to independence. Thus the whole shape of the international system today is largely derived from nationalism and the effects of nationalist movements (Mayall, 1990).

At the same time, international relations and the structure of international society have an impact on nationalism, and they often determine its success or failure and the form which it takes. The foreign policy of a state tends to be conducive of national unity and nationalism, since party differences are often laid aside in the name of patriotism. So nationalism both affects international relations, and is affected by it.

Nationalism and International Conflict

Nationalism is still regarded as a major threat to peace today, despite the satisfaction of many of its demands. For a time after 1945, other divisions between states appeared as important as those derived from nationalism. The 'Cold War' split many states along ideological lines (communist/non-communist) in blocs which superseded the confines of the nation-state. International bodies such as the United Nations and the European Economic Community gave an institutional expression to supranationalism, and multinational firms operated with scant regard to nation-state boundaries or national loyalties. But all this was not an indication of the 'end of nationalism', even if it showed that an alternative to nationalism was available. By the 1960s, nationalism showed that it was once more the greatest threat to international peace, with Islamic fundamentalism next in importance. The strong affinities between nationalism and Islamic fundamentalism make it sometimes difficult to tell them apart, and perhaps the latter is really another indication of the revival of nationalism (Halliday and Alavi, 1988).

According to Joseph Rothschild, 'politicised ethnicity has become the most keen and potent edge of intrastate and interstate conflict, displacing class and ideological conflict, and it asserts itself today, dialectically, as the leading legitimator or delegitimating challenger of political authority' (Rothschild, 1981, p. 31).

Evidence to support this statement with regard to *intrastate* conflict has been given in the preceding chapters. In this chapter attention is focused on *interstate* (international) conflict, and 'politicised ethnicity' is broadened to include all types of nationalism in international relations.

Contemporary political conflicts relating to nationalism which involve more than one state are to be found in many places: in the Middle East (Israel and the Arab states; the Kurds and Turkey, Iraq and Iran, Iraq and Kuwait, Saudi Arabia, etc); in Eastern Europe (the former 'satellite' states and the USSR, and Germany's relations with Poland and the USSR); in Northern Ireland (the Republic of Ireland and Britain); in the Indian sub-continent (Pakistan and India over Kashmir; India and Sri Lanka); and so on. The character of such conflicts between states varies from armed warfare to peaceful negotiation, even institutional cooperation, as in the 'Anglo–Irish Agreement' and the Indian Army's invited presence in Sri Lanka from 1987 to 1989. In some cases, conflict between states is a result of a nationalism which is not directly sponsored by the states themselves, and which may be embarrassing to them. Thus Kurdish nationalism has led to conflicts between Turkey, Iraq, and Iran, but it is also directed against these states. Similarly, Irish nationalism in Northern Ireland has led to tension between Britain and the Republic of Ireland, although the Irish Republican Army and Sinn Fein oppose the governments of both states. Britain and Ireland are drawn into the conflict as reluctant proxies for both sides in the struggle in Northern Ireland.

The study of nationalism in international relations is confusing because it deals at times with *states* and at other times with *nations*, *nationalities* and *ethnic groups*, none of which are states. In the context of interstate relations, nationalism is contrasted with 'internationalism' and 'supranationalism'. States are described as 'nationalist' or 'internationalist' according to their political behaviour. Nationalist political behaviour is characterised as ethnocentrism, aggressive patriotism ('jingoism'), and imperialism. Suspicion of, and antipathy to, other states, a desire to preserve 'national sovereignty', aggressive behaviour with a desire to dominate or colonise other states or peoples, make up the gamut of official (state) nationalism in international relations. 'Internationalism', by contrast, means the pursuit of interstate cooperation, with 'supranationalism' being the subordination of state sovereignty in international institutions such as the United Nations and the European Community.

Nation-states and Multinational states in International Relations

So far in this treatment of nationalism, no assumptions have been made about the internal national or ethnic composition of the state, for the term 'nation' has been used as the equivalent of the state (as in the United Nations). Even 'ethnocentrism' in international relations does not imply a basis in ethnicity as we have discussed it earlier. Instead it relates to the nationalist behaviour of the citizens or of the government of the state.

In the second usage of nationalism in international relations, referring to nations as distinct from states, there is a closer correspondence to the 'ethnic' and 'social' types discussed earlier in this book. Now nationalism can be found in opposition to official nationalism or patriotism. Moreover, it is possible to consider whether the internal national and ethnic composition of states is important in international relations. It can be asked whether the stability of the state system is affected by the degree of national or ethnic homogeneity which each state possesses. Where a state largely comprises a socially homogeneous nation it can be clearly called a 'nation-state', but such states are comparatively rare, despite efforts at 'nation-building'.

It is worth considering whether it is true that the nearer a state comes to social and ethnic homogeneity, the less it is likely to engage in 'nationalist' activity in international relations. There is evidence that internal national unity and the successful realisation of a nation-state produces stability and moderates the nationalism of a state's foreign policy. A state which is nationally and ethnically disunited may seek to divert attention from its internal problems by pursuing nationalist activities externally. So the internal and external aspects of nationalism are linked together.

Since most states are not social or ethnic nation-states, either because of their multinational character, or because the members of the nation are spread across more than one state, the potential for nationalist behaviour in international relations is great. The extent and intensity of such behaviour is linked to the degree of internal disunity, especially ethnic, and to unsatisfied claims for national unification (*irredentism*).

'Official nationalism' (the nationalism of states) is thus largely dependent on the degree of 'social nationalism' shared by all citizens. States must become social nations if they are to mobilise nationalist behaviour successfully and amongst all the population. This poses a dilemma for multinational states such as the USSR and even Britain, for the only way to produce an overall official nationalism out of several social nationalisms is to subordinate or suppress these nationalisms within the state. Thus 'Soviet patriotism' must override Russian national feeling, and British patriotism must predominate over appeals to English national pride. In times of supreme crisis, however, as during the Second World War, there is to be seen a reversion to social and ethnic nationalism as the most powerful loyalty when a supreme sacrifice is required. Thus Russian and English nationalism proved more effective in mobilising support in Russia and England than the state-based Soviet and British patriotism.

This shows that the existence in one state of several social nationalisms, and even more so, ethnic nationalisms or exclusive nationalisms, makes official nationalism difficult to sustain. The reaction of minority nations against majority nationalism is often a destabilising force constituting an 'enemy within' the state. Ukrainians proved unreliable allies of the Russians in the Second World War and the Irish virtually broke away from the British in the First World War.

The reaction of multinational states to social and ethnic nationalism is often to become authoritarian, perhaps with military rule. This type of regime can draw on some support from the minority nations, especially if the army and government are multinational in composition, but it will not mobilise support for official nationalism if it is seen to be in reality the exclusive nationalism of the majority nation. Many Scots and Ukrainians identified with 'England' and 'Russia' respectively in times of war as they were an integral part of the army and were not excluded from power at the centre. But in the First World War it was impossible to mobilise many Irish in support of the British state, for they had always been largely power-less at the centre of the state. In the Second World War the Baltic nations annexed to the USSR in 1940 were considered unreliable supporters of the Soviet state. Many of their citizens were deported to Siberia by Stalin, as were 'ethnic Germans' in the Soviet Union. Today, most citizens of the Baltic nations wish to secede from the USSR.

Of course, the ethnic composition of a state is not the only guide to its power and foreign policy. Writers on international relations have analysed the elements of power at length, and most concentrate on fac-tors such as the size of the population, territory, economic resources, the army, and the quality of leadership. Few have considered how national homogeneity or heterogeneity affect state power and foreign policy. Yet there is strong evidence that these are as important as the other variables in the equation. Counterbalancing this, there is much scope for governments to appeal to patriotism and hatred of foreigners, and here 'official' nationalism is posed against 'social' and 'ethnic' nationalism. Internal party and ethnic divisions tend to disappear when support for the state's foreign policy is involved, especially in times of war. But even so, 'official' nationalism is weaker than the other types, as was seen in the break-up of the Austrian and Ottoman Empires in 1918. There is no space to pursue this hypothesis further here, and we must turn to other aspects of nationalism in international relations.

'Nationals' and 'Citizens'

'Nationality' (citizenship) rights can be a problem in international affairs. Most states prefer their citizens to be members of a homo-geneous nation, and their immigration laws reflect this. Automatic rights of citizenship are typically offered to those deemed to be co-nationals , and exclusions are drawn up for those considered 'aliens'. The aim is usually to maintain a 'social' or even 'ethnic' nation, made up of people who resemble each other culturally and ethnically. The further a person is from that norm the less likely is it that that person will gain admission to the state.

Britain has immigration laws which give no automatic right of residence to holders of British passports, unless they have a parent or grandparent who was born in Britain. Some states give perpetual rights of entry to those considered 'nationals', even if they have been citizens of other states for many years, even centuries. This shows the ethnic nationalism of these states, and the desire to satisfy the 'nation-state' principle. Thus the Constitution of the Federal Republic of Germany (West Germany) gave automatic citizenship to German immigrants from the German Democratic Republic (East Germany), and even from Poland and the Soviet Union (the 'Volga Germans' returning to West Germany in the 1980s had left Germany to settle in Russia in the eighteenth century!). The Republic of Ireland grants Irish citizenship to the residents of Northern Ireland, which in international law is part of Britain. Such residents may therefore hold two passports. Israel promises a National Home to all Jews under its Law of Return, and Switzerland recognises as Swiss anyone with a Swiss ancestor (but this is not common ethnicity).

In contrast, the further a potential immigrant is from the national ideal the more difficult it is to gain entry. When Uganda expelled its Asian citizens in 1971, those who chose British citizenship found that their British passports did not entitle them to automatic entry to Britain, but only to join a queue to qualify under a quota. They thus became almost 'stateless persons'. Technically 'colour-blind' immigration rules in Britain, the United States, and France mask discrimination against black immigrants. 'Grandfather clauses' (as in the British Immigration Act 1971), work permits, and property and wealth qualifications effectively exclude immigrants who are unwelcome on ethnic grounds. The justification for these regulations takes the form of a variety of rationalisations and evasions concerning the 'problems' which such immigrants introduce into the social fabric of the state. In essence, they assert that form of nationalism (social and ethnic) in which homogeneity of 'culture' (a euphemism for ethnicity and colour) is valued above a 'multicultural' society.

The international aspect of this is that there may be a conflict between states about their rights of citizenship and their treatment of refugees. Hungary and West Germany were criticised by East Germany in 1989 for encouraging a mass exodus of East Germans to West Germany through Hungary. The restriction on entry to Britain of refugees from Uganda and Hong Kong, and of the entry of the 'Vietnamese boat people' to Hong Kong, Japan and the United States are further examples of how citizenship rights impinge on international relations.

Nationalism, Internationalism and Supranationalism

States form the foundation of the international system, which is in reality a club of states. The United Nations Charter (Article 2) protects the sovereignty of its members ('no interference in the domestic jurisdiction of any state'), and has not supported the break-up of a state by a nationalist movement. At the same time, the Charter proclaims (Article 1) the 'principle of equal rights and self-determination of peoples', and its International Covenant on Civil and Political Rights (1966) states that 'All peoples have the right of self-determination. By virtue of that right they freely determine their political status and freely pursue their economic, social and cultural development' (Article 1). In practice, 'peoples' has meant colonial peoples whose self-determination from the European empires has been backed by the UN. The rights of national 'minorities', which were a major concern of the League of Nations in the 1920s and 1930s, have not similarly occupied the attention of the United Nations after 1945, with the exception of the Palestinians in Israel, whose claims have been supported by the General Assembly. Thus the state system outside the colonies has hardened and it is in vain that the nationalists of 'unrepresented nations' such as Scotland and the Basque lands appeal to the UN to support their 'right of national self-determination'.

The European Community (EC) is a more complex international institution than the UN, with laws which have direct force in the member states. To that extent, it can be called a 'supranational' body. The process of 'integration' of states into international and supranational bodies is a part of the study of international relations, giving rise to 'integration theory' (e.g., Haas, 1958 and Mitrany, 1975). This seeks to predict the political unification of states and nations from 'functional cooperation' in international bodies such as the European Economic Community. Others predict integration through increased social communication, as in Deutsch's theory of nation-building (Deutsch, 1953). There are also political propagandists for integration, as in the European Movement.

Despite these analyses and predictions, 'integration theory' failed to live up to expectations. 'Functional cooperation' and increased communication did not lead to full supranationalism, although the European Community did develop a 'Single European Market' and the increased use of 'majority voting' in the Council of Ministers. Yet nationalism of all kinds is involved in the politics of the EC. Some Governments of the member states have acted in a nationalist way, defending their sovereignty against supranationalism. Thus De Gaulle in the 1960s proclaimed that the EC was a *'Europe des patries'* with members retaining the right to veto decisions they considered were against their national interests. In September 1988, Margaret Thatcher's speech at Bruges was a latter-day attack on moves towards a 'United States of Europe'. For her, each state in the EC had to preserve its own traditions, 'a sense of national pride in one's own country', and it would be 'folly to try to fit them into some sort of identikit European personality' (*The Scotsman*, 21 September 1988).

Thatcher was responding to the plans to further integrate the EC in a Single European Market by 1992, which her Government had already agreed to. Her nationalism is reflected in the attitude of British public opinion to the EC, which differs markedly from that in the other member states. In 1987, only 46% of British respondents in the *Eurobarometer* survey thought membership of the EC a 'good thing', and only 24% were 'very much' in favour of efforts to unite Western Europe (Commission of the European Communities: *Eurobarometer*, no. 28, December 1987, pp. B63, B48). In this survey, people in the member states of the EC ranged widely in their attitudes to European unity. Only 29% of Danes thought the Single European Market was a 'good thing', followed by 43% for the British. At the other end of the scale, 77% of the Irish were in favour, followed by 66% of the Belgians (*ibid.*, p .36). It would be rash to conclude from this that the Irish are the least nationalist nation in western Europe, since the context here covers only one aspect of nationalism. The Irish were, and to some extent still are, fiercely nationalist in their relations with Britain. But their nationalism is not opposed to the supranationalism of the European Community. As a small nation, their position is actually enhanced through membership of the EC, which gives them a stage and a status which they would not otherwise possess. As important, they perceive their economic interests to be strongly served by membership of the EC.

For the British, however, Thatcher's emphasis on 'national pride' and a separate culture points to a more traditional form of nationalism shared by much of the population. As a large state with an imperial past, and continuing aspirations to Great Power status, Britain might suffer a diminution of power in the EC, in which Germany and France are dominant. The economic benefits of EC membership are more disputed in Britain, although most business interests back the economic unification of Europe, as do liberal internationalists.

The support for the EC now shown by the Scottish and Welsh nationalists, and by the Basques, Catalans and Corsicans, etc, is a further dimension to 'internationalism'. Here, opposition to the centralised states of which these nations are part is coupled with a desire to be represented in the European Community. As with the Irish, these nationalists have come to see the EC as an opportunity to play a part on a wider stage and to influence EC decisions, either in a 'Europe of the Regions' or as new member states. They hope thereby to make gains for their nations which are unlikely to come to them from the existing states' monopoly of the EC decision-making process. That is because they see the interests of the states as different from those of their nations.

Some nationalists (e.g., the SNP) seek sovereign statehood within the EC. How this can be reconciled with the subsequent loss of sovereignty in a supranational EC is a puzzle which has not escaped those nationalists who have opposed membership of the EC on the grounds that national independence would be sacrificed in a vast political organisation which is dominated by multinational economic interests and a remote bureaucracy (the Scottish Green Party takes the same view). In reply, the SNP says it seeks a reconstructed 'confederal' Europe rather than a supranational one.

Ethnocentrism and Xenophobia in International Relations

The attitudes of the people of a nation towards other nations can easily become ethnocentric and even xenophobic, even if no obvious political hostility exists between them. Thus 36% of the respondents in Britain in a 1984 MORI survey (*The Sunday Times*, 19 June 1984) regarded France 'unfavourably' and 33% of those in France in turn regarded

Table 10.1 *'Net favourability' of attitudes in Britain and France towards other countries*

Towards:	In Britain %	In France %
Switzerland	+76	+60
Sweden	+73	+58
West Germany	+55	+44
USA	+45	+41
Italy	+31	+42
Japan	+26	+28
Spain	+24	+37
Portugal	+30	+44
Greece	+25	+47
France	+8	-
China	+21	+17
Poland	+11	+52
Israel	−1	+24
Soviet Union	−48	−39
Algeria	−24	−2
UK	-	+5

Source: surveys as above, quoted in Nancy J. Walker and Robert M. Worcester, 'Nationalism in Britain', unpublished paper for International Political Science Association Congress, Paris, July 1985.

Britain 'unfavourably' (IFOP survey in *Le Nouvel Observateur*, 8 June 1984). Only the Soviet Union, in a list of 15 countries, was more unfavourably regarded in France (54%), and that was repeated in Britain (62%). The country regarded most favourably in Britain and France was Switzerland, which perhaps indicates that its political neutrality makes it attractive to the citizens of other nations. Yet one might expect allies such as Britain and France to rate each other more highly than a neutral state. It is likely that more widespread hostile nationalist attitudes are involved in the relations between the British and the French.

It is interesting to compare the attitudes of the British and the French to a range of other states. Subtracting the 'unfavourable' attitudes from the 'favourable' gives the results shown in Table 10.1.

A similar survey, conducted by the *New York Times* (November 10, 1985), on attitudes in the US towards the 'Russians', Germans, British and Japanese, found that 56% of respondents said the Russians were 'quite different' from Americans. Only 38% said the Japanese were 'quite different'. That current political differences largely determine attitudes is seen by the large number of respondents (44%) who did not know that the Soviet Union and the United States had fought on the same side in the Second World War; 28% thought that the countries had actually fought against each other! Anti-Soviet attitudes were fostered at this time in 'Rambo'-type films and in the media, sport, etc, and President Reagan for a time referred to the USSR as an 'evil empire'. Politicians find it relatively easy to play on nationalist attitudes in their conduct of international relations. In times of war, such sentiments quickly become xenophobic. At the same time, it seems that a change to peaceful political relationships, such as the end of conflict between the US and Japan, leads to favourable popular attitudes developing. Conversely, the Soviet Union, an ally of the US in the Second World War, became the object of xenophobia during the Cold War. The relaxation of tension under Gorbachev will likely be reflected in a lower level of mutually hostile nationalism in both countries.

Ethnic groups and foreign policy

In some countries, ethnic groups have an important influence in the formulation of a state's foreign policy. Often this influence is dispro-portionate to the size of the group. For example, the Jewish population of the US is around 4% of the total, yet it has been largely responsible for aligning the US strongly behind Israel. Indeed, Israel receives more foreign aid from the US than any other state, and would probably disintegrate without such support.

There are several reasons for the strength of the Jewish lobby in the US. Specially significant is the political influence which comes from the great wealth of the Jewish community. This is important since American politics is financed and largely controlled by private interests. But there is also a general sympathy with the state of Israel as a home for refugees from Hitler's Europe. As an immigrant nation itself, with many of its Jews the victims of Hitler, the US is psychologically and philosophically similar to Israel. Where it tends to break with Israel is over the latter's repressive policies towards the Palestinians. Yet it is a sign of the strength of the Jewish lobby in the US that aid to Israel has been maintained at its high level even when the interests of the US might have been more profitably served by alliance with the Arab states, who cut oil supplies to the US during their wars with Israel in the 1960s and 1970s. States with a weak Jewish lobby, such as Britain, France and the Netherlands, are much more likely to take the Arab side or to be neutral in such wars. The 1956 Suez intervention by Britain and France on the side of Israel was based on self-interest rather than on support for Israel.

Ethnic groups which are active politically in international relations but do not have the support of the governments of their states are usually those whose aims are subversive of the governments of other states. The 'Club of States' is unlikely to encourage nationalists who seek to dismember one of its members. Thus international support for the secessionist nations in the USSR and Yugoslavia has been muted, or limited to 'moral support'. Again, although many Irish-Americans support the Irish Republicans in Northern Ireland, the US Government is careful to distance itself from the Irish nationalist cause. This has not prevented the US Congress sustaining an Irish lobby of Congressmen sympathetic to the IRA and Sinn Fein. But 'Noraid', an organisation which raises money in the US for Irish nationalists in Northern Ireland, is not an official organisation, and the US Government tries to prevent assistance going to the IRA. At the same time, Irish-American politicians such as President Ronald Reagan and Senator Edward Kennedy have shown more sympathy towards the Nationalist community in Northern Ireland than towards the Loyalist community. This has been a source of some tension in US–British relations.

Ethnic groups in countries other than the US are generally weaker in their influence over foreign policy. In part, that is because such groups are not usually immigrants with a close interest in their country of origin. Rather, they are likely to be natives whose political demands relate solely to their own state. We have seen that in some cases *irredentism* may involve interstate relations, as between Britain and Ireland, and in these countries lobbies exist to press the cases of the nationalists and anti-nationalists. However, no British party in recent times until 1990 operated in Northern Ireland, which means that the Irish nationalists and Unionists have to influence the British Government at second hand through sympathisers in the British parties, or through the small Northern Irish parties which are excluded from government. In the Republic of Ireland, support for nationalism in Northern Ireland is muted, and the Government of Ireland has sought cooperation with the British Government in addition to its general support for Irish nationalism in the North. The IRA is banned in the Republic of Ireland, so that only moderate nationalism gets the overt support of the Irish Government. This has not prevented the IRA drawing aid from some people in the South, and IRA fugitives escape to the Republic of Ireland to evade the British authorities.

The role of ethnic groups in shaping a state's foreign policy thus derives from their influence in the political system of that country, and from the congruence between the interests of the state and the interests of the groups. A multiethnic state based on immigrants is likely to have more involvement in nationalisms abroad than a non-immigrant multinational state. A political system with a non-disciplined party system and dependent on private funding, such as that of the US, gives greater scope for ethnic political influence than those such as Britain or France, with greater party discipline and less private funding. But in nearly all states ethnic groups have a significant, if often hidden, influence in the making of foreign policy.

11

Conclusion: An Integrated Theory of the Politics of Nationalism and Ethnicity

An integrated or general theory of the politics of nationalism and ethnicity must be the aim of all students of the subject. Without such a theory, it is impossible to make a claim that understanding has been advanced beyond the level of the description and partial analysis of apparently unrelated case studies.

Of course, such a theory is far from easy to formulate, and it has in fact eluded most scholars so far. Writers on nationalism and ethnicity sometimes even deny the possibility of such a theory (Breuilly, 1982, p. 2), or deliberately avoid attempting one (Keating, 1988, p. viii). Those works which are overtly theoretical sometimes provide a selection of theories from which the reader can choose, but in which there is no integration into one theory (e.g., Rex and Mason (eds), 1986). The theories in Rex and Mason include sociobiology, Marxism, Weberian forms of class analysis, plural society theory, and 'rational choice theory' (*ibid.*, pp. ix–xiii).

In this book, account is also taken of such theories, but an attempt is made to construct one integrated or general theory out of those theories which seem to be consistent with one another, and which are otherwise convincing. This of course is no guarantee that the theory so constructed will be correct or even the best available. Even if all the consistent and convincing parts of current theories were put together, the end result could still be wrong. Moreover, the exercise could be considered merely eclectic, not original. But even on that interpretation (which I would not accept), the resulting theory is worthwhile if it is able to explain the main phenomena in the subject.

The claim made here is that although this 'integrated theory' is built upon the works of others, its originality lies in combining these into a general theory in which the 'building-blocks' are clearly displayed, and in which 'necessary' and 'sufficient' conditions for aspects of the politics of nationalism and ethnicity are identified. Each successive building-block is built on its predecessor, so that the later building-blocks follow on from the earlier ones. Within each building-block are identified those features which are assessed as either 'necessary' or 'sufficient' conditions for certain aspects of the politics of nationalism and ethnicity.

Objections to the validity of one or more of the building-blocks and to the assessment of the 'conditions' are inevitable, given that most theorists deny the truth of theories other than their own. But even if it can be shown that a particular part of the theory is wrong, this should not destroy the validity of the whole theory, although it may alter some of its character. In this there is an analogy between the relative compatibility of quantum physics and Newtonian physics. In some aspects, one seems to contradict the other, yet at different levels of analysis both are correct. Thus, in this integrated theory, sociobiological theory may seem incompatible with contextualist or historic theory, yet both theories are trying to answer different questions.

At the least, the attempt to produce such an integrated theory should stimulate debate about the viability of such an endeavour, and provide a much-needed general framework for the study of the mass of evidence relating to the politics of nationalism and ethnicity. At the end of the chapter, a synopsis of the theory is provided in which the building-blocks are clearly indicated.

The Theory

An integrated theory of the politics of nationalism and ethnicity must begin with human nature, for there is strong evidence that innate and instinctive forces are at work in ethnic identification and ethnocentric behaviour (Chapter 1). Ethnocentrism is a type of behaviour which may be genetically determined, although the evidence for this from sociobiology is controversial. Even if sociobiological theories regarding ethnocentrism are rejected, we still have to explain what causes this form of human behaviour, and its peculiarly intense emotional appeal. In politics, nationalism and ethnicity often represent supreme loyalties overpowering other political divisions. In no other type of politics has there been so much violence, warfare and death. Theorists who exclude human nature from their scheme of things must find an alternative explanation for this phenomenon. Contextualists, for example, will argue that nationalism is a modern phenomenon, and therefore cannot relate to 'universal' human nature. They will point to the 'pre-national' violence in wars of religion, imperialism, and so on, which match those relating to nationalism and ethnicity today. It is certainly true that nationalism has no monopoly of violence or emotion, and that most of its political features today are the result of comparatively recent history. Yet its essential basis is in ethnocentrism, which has existed long before nationalism emerged as an ideology. This must make us consider the biological and psychological aspects of the subject.

In this theory, certain features of human nature provide the sufficient conditions for ethnocentrism, but it is not yet clear why that should be so. The theoretical explanation is in part found in sociobiology. Some sociobiologists claim that ethnocentrism is a genetically-determined behaviour in which 'kin selection' operates. This means that kin are preferred to non-kin as mates, and that the 'inclusive fitness' of kin groups is the result. This theory can explain ethnic social bonding, and if correct, can provide necessary or sufficient conditions for xenophobia, nepotism, slavery and genocide (van den Berghe, 1981). The sociobiological 'building-block' of the theory of nationalism and ethnicity presented here is perhaps the most controversial of all its components. Many will reject any connection between biology and political behaviour, especially nationalist behaviour. The evidence is inconclusive, but the balance seems to be in favour of a link between ethnocentrism and human instincts (see Reynolds *et al.* (eds), 1987). That is why this 'building-block' is retained.

Another input to the study of nationalism has come from neurophysiology. Some neurophysiologists have related particular languages to particular types of brain (e.g., Japanese brains cope best with the Japanese language, etc). The implication is that language and biology are linked, and that 'mother tongues' are the most 'natural'. Most experts on socio-linguistics would reject this view (e.g., Fishman, 1971–2, 1973, 1985), and would stress instead the social and political determinants of language use and survival. What seems incontrovertible is that neurophysiological factors are necessary conditions for language and are sufficient to produce 'mother tongues'. These languages have a peculiar potency, which subsequent language shifts cannot totally erase. Total bilingualism (or trilingualism, etc) seems to be extremely rare. Some theorists seeks to relate linguistic nationalism (unilingualism) to human nature. At present, there seems to be little hard evidence to support that conclusion, and it is retained here for reference rather than as one of the essential parts of a theory of nationalism.

What is essential for any theory of nationalism is an explanation of its emotional appeal, and of the virulence of ethnocentrism. Why should strong feelings of loyalty to one's nation or ethnic group develop, along with equally strong hatreds of foreigners? Here, a study of social psychology is required to explain how group behaviour is determined. It seems to be a sufficient condition of 'ingroup' and 'outgroup' hostility that these groups be clearly defined, even if they have only been artificially constructed in the laboratory. If the groups are based on instinctive (biological) divisions or on language divisions this is likely to heighten ingroup/outgroup hostility. A language division between groups is an obvious source of annoyance, since it may mean the inability to communicate. Ascriptive (especially visible) group differences such as those of skin colour, facial appearance, etc, will also increase the likelihood of heightened group hostility.

Conflicts between groups may be considered 'realistic' if they are based on the pursuit of their members' 'rational self-interest'. For example, it may be rational for speakers of a particular language to seek the reservation of jobs in the government for speakers of that language. 'Irrational' group conflict, on the other hand, results from pathological feelings of displacement and frustration, and is often purely destructive, with no chance of gain to the group. Thus much of the violence and killing associated with nationalism can be traced to psychological stress, especially feelings of insecurity. Of course, this leaves unexplained what caused that stress and insecurity in the first place. This can only be discovered from the political context. What is explained here is the psychology of the response to some types of division between nations and ethnic groups.

The translation of a kin group into an ethnic group and of an ethnic group into a nation is essentially a matter of the subjective perceptions of members of the group, rather than an instinctive phenomenon. Even a kin group may be subjective in social terms, for the perception of relatedness within it may not correspond to an actual biological relationship. It may be 'fictive kin'. When one moves to ethnic and national identity the importance of perceptions and ideas becomes more obvious. 'Objective' criteria of ethnicity and nationality such as language and religion are social rather than instinctive or psychological in origin. And such criteria are never sufficient to explain entirely the existence of particular ethnic groups and nations, or particular forms of ethnocentrism and nationalism. It is the perception of ethnicity and nationhood by its members which determines the ethnic group/nation's political existence and behaviour.

This perception results from an idea (of the nation, ethnic group, or race) and from ideologies associated with that idea (nationalism, racism, etc) (Chapter 2). These are necessary to the idea of the nation and, later, sufficient to produce an ideology of nationalism. Where these ideas and ideologies came from, and when, has preoccupied the minds of many writers on nationalism. Despite a near-consensus amongst them that the idea of nationalism originated in the French Revolution at the end of the 18th century, the evidence shows that it is much older. It took hold at different times in history in different places. Some nationalisms date back to the distant past (e.g., Jewish nationalism – but not Zionism, a 19th century construction), while others are still in the process of formation. It is true that a philosophical justification for nationalism had to await the 19th century, and many of the ideas propounded at that time were new (e.g., linguistic nationalism and democratic nationalism). Fascism, Nazism and Apartheid are examples of 20th century ideologies of racism and nationalism. So the idea of the nation and the ideology of nationalism have been evolving over many centuries. What is important for the theory of nationalism and ethnicity is that an essential building-block for it is the role of ideas and ideologies. These determine the transition from ethnocentrism to ethnicity and to nationhood, and from ethnocentrism and ethnic loyalty to nationalism.

The reason why these ideas and ideologies came to be formulated, and the explanation for their strengths and weaknesses in different circumstances, is a matter of considerable speculation among theorists. An interaction of political, economic and cultural factors is involved, playing on the presumed 'givens' of biology and psychology (Chapters 3 and 4). Among the many sources of nations and nationalism which have been detected, at least in its earlier phases, are: the progressive **political** centralisation of state authority, with the breakdown of local loyalties and the weakening of cosmopolitan religions; the coming of democracy; **economic** and social change, especially industrialisation; and **cultural** change after the invention of printing, especially the development of 'national' languages and national education systems, shaping people into nations.

It is difficult to say which of these developments are exclusively or even closely associated with nationalism. There is an ambiguity about the effect of all of them, with nationalism only one possible outcome. For example, there seems to be no inherent reason why democracy should lead to nations and nationalism rather than to multinational or even supranational political authorities and loyalties. Indeed, some people seek 'world government', or at least 'European Union' on a democratic basis. Printing, too, might just as easily lead to an international language as to national languages. Today, English is becoming such a language. Industrialisation may have accompanied the rise of the nation-state in continental Europe, but it is weakly associated with nationalism (and even less with ethnic politics) in the recent history of the British Isles and in the nationalisms of the contemporary Third World.

At this point, theorising becomes difficult and unsatisfactory. Some writers refuse to try, proclaiming each case 'unique'. This is surely unhelpful. Each case is of course to some extent unique, but all have features in common which relate to the building-blocks of the theory. A sovereign state is necessary for a 'nation-state', and sufficient to produce 'official nationalism'. Democracy and social homogeneity in the state lead to a merging of official nationalism with 'social nationalism'. Conversely, national inequalities and displacements in a multinational state or empire provide the conditions for 'ethnic nationalism'.

Particularly relevant are the types of political, economic and social differences among ethnic groups and nations. These may be the result of unintended 'uneven economic development' or of deliberate political and economic discrimination through 'internal colonialism'. What emerges is a 'cultural (or ethnic) division of labour' in which ethnic groups occupy distinct economic and political positions in society. Such a situation is a necessary (and even sufficient) condition for 'ethnic nationalism', especially if national or ethnic groups are treated unequally in the state and perceive themselves to be exploited. An ethnic-based disjunction between economic and political power so that the group which controls the state is relatively weak in the economy (or vice versa) also heightens nationalism in the weaker group. A rapid change in the balance of these economic and political forces is the situation which is most likely to produce a nationalist reaction.

All this links again into the psychology of nationalism. Thwarted expectations lead to displacement and frustration, with a strong desire to express resentment against an outgroup. When the ingroups and outgroups are defined as ethnic or national and there is also a cultural division of labour, the scene is set for strong nationalist political behaviour if the capability to do so is present.

This is only one possible context for nationalist political behaviour. Another recurring context is a threat to, or displacement of, the boundaries of the nation. Such boundaries may be social and economic as well as territorial. Immigration may be such a threat, with the fear of a dilution of national homogeneity and the displacement of nationals from economic and political jobs. This is a strong theme in the 'nationality question' in the Soviet Union. A similar threat is that of assimilation to another nation, as in the 'Russification' of the non-Russian nations. So group 'boundary maintenance' is closely related to nationalism.

In the advanced industrial societies (or 'post-industrial societies') nationalism is linked to the spread of 'post-materialist values'. These values stress the quality of life rather than economic interests. Those who divide along nationalist lines rather than along lines of social class in these societies are often 'post-materialists'. If they vote for nationalist parties, they weaken the class-based parties. Nationalist and Green parties in western Europe and Popular Fronts in the Soviet Union are supported by citizens whose political concerns are with the environment and with constitutional freedoms, and they express these concerns through nationalism rather than through class politics. So 'post-industrial society' provides the conditions for the development of new types of nationalist and ethnic politics.

The introduction of political parties and other political organisations into the theory of nationalism changes the focus to the operation of politics *per se* (Chapter 5). Here a complex interaction of forces is involved, with nationalist parties in competition not only with non-nationalist parties, but often among themselves in rival nationalist parties and organisations. Their ability to operate freely and to appeal successfully to the electorate varies greatly from case to case. While the political appeal of nationalism depends largely on the general social and economic context in which it operates, its practical success in politics is strongly related to leadership, organisation, and the vagaries of the political climate.

Voting for nationalist parties is only one dimension of nationalist political behaviour, and it usually understates the strength of nationalism. Non-nationalist parties often use nationalist appeals in order to pre-empt the nationalists' campaign. Nationalist leaders are drawn from particular sections of the nation, and are not socially representative of the nation as a whole. They use nationalism and ethnicity as a political resource to gain election and political rewards, and their success depends on the relative weakness of other political leaders to project non-nationalist issues as the most important.

Where social class divisions are weak or politically unmobilised (as in the Third World countries), or are being replaced by sectional and post-industrial politics (as in many developed countries), nationalist or ethnic parties can be important. The nationalists' capacity to compete with other political leaders depends on the total configuration of politics, especially the power exerted by the state. Unfortunately, this part of the theory is unable to predict particular outcomes for nationalist parties and movements without either indulging in tautology or getting immersed in a mass of detail peculiar to particular cases (Chapters 6, 7, and 8).

A brief taxonomy of the types of nationalism indicates the complexity of the subject, when actual cases are studied:

Table 11.1 *Types of nationalism*

Historic

(i)   *Pre-19th century.* State to nation (nation-building): e.g., England, Scotland, France, Portugal. Colonial nationalism.

(ii) *19th–early 20th century.* Nation to state (national unification or independence): e.g., Germany, Italy, Ireland.

(iii) *Post-1945 anti-colonial nationalism* (India, Ghana, etc).

(iv) *Post-industrial developed world nationalism*, e.g., Scottish, Flemish, Quebecois)

(v)   *Post-independence, i.e. 1947–ncommunal nationalism in Third World* (e.g., Kashmir, Punjab, Biafra, Sri Lanka).

(vi) *Post-authoritarian regime nationalism* (e.g., Catalan, Basque, Soviet Republics).

Geographic

(i)   *Europe:* home of 'classical' and now 'post-industrial' nationalism (seen in west European capitalist countries and central/east European communist or ex-communist countries).

(ii) *Colonial or European settler countries* (e.g., Latin-America, the United States, Canada, Australia, South Africa, Israel).

(iii) Third World: African and Asian anti-colonial nationalism, 'pan-' movements, ethnic politics and communalism.

Forms and intensity (in ascending order of violence)

(i) Cultural: generally confined to intellectuals, but language conflicts can affect wider populations (especially, in Belgium, Quebec, Soviet republics, Yugoslavia).

(ii) Constitutional: in democratic systems, nationalist parties and movements which peacefully campaign for national self-determination, relying mainly on votes in elections and referendums (e.g., Scotland, Catalonia, Lithuania). Also, nationalists or autonomists who accept the multinational state or consociational democracy (Belgium, Catalonia, Quebec).

(iii) Peaceful direct action: conventions, plebiscites and declarations of independence outside the constitutional process (e.g., Ireland before 1921, Scotland, Quebec, Lithuania).

(iv) Violent direct action: (e.g., 'terrorist' or paramilitary groups (Quebec FLQ, Basque ETA, Corsican FNLC, Irish IRA).

(v) Communal violence: especially found in Third World countries (e.g., Nigeria, India, Sri Lanka, Fiji, etc), but also in 'settler' countries (South Africa, Israel), and in urban areas of industrialised countries in the form of racial violence (e.g., the US and Britain).

Despite the complexity of this taxonomy, some generalisations can be given. No theory of nationalist politics can be based on a 'bottom-up' approach alone which looks just at the activities of the nationalists themselves. A 'top-down' analysis is also necessary to explain how those who hold the power at the centre act in a context of subversive nationalism. 'Official nationalism' (patriotism) is used by states to combat the nationalism of 'ethnic' and 'social' nationalists who seek to dismember the state. Such an appeal to patriotism is especially effective in international relations, and can divert attention from the other nationalisms within the state.

Anti-state nationalist movements are weak until an overall 'regime change' takes place. Then their capacity to overturn the political system is enhanced. Such regime changes occur rarely, however, and are usually the result of war, revolution, or the death of a dictator. Thus ethnic nationalists in Spain, Yugoslavia and the Soviet Union found themselves suddenly with the capacity to achieve some measure of national independence when autocratic governments were replaced with more liberal regimes, which proceeded to decentralise power.

The ability of nationalists to form credible parties and to conduct government successfully is a subsequent test of the strength of nationalism. Nationalist parties get caught up in politics generally, and sometimes become governing parties. Their nationalism may be insufficient to win continuing support from the electorate if they fail to act sensibly and, if in government, to satisfy economic and social demands. Nations are rarely united politically, and nationalist parties are exposed to the problems which other parties face – poor leadership, division, and the threat of dissolution by an intolerant state. Divided nations and divided nationalist movements are normal, and this gives much scope for anti-nationalist forces to 'divide and rule'. Only where the perception of national oppression is great will the nationalist movement override such opposition.

A branch of the theory of the politics of nationalism and ethnicity is the study of the politics of multiethnic states (Chapter 9). So too are the strategies for political accommodation in ethnically 'divided societies', and especially the theory of *consociational democracy* (Chapter 9). These concern alternatives to the nation-state in the form of a multinational democracy based on the equal partnership of several nations within one state. In one version, consociational democracy is presented as a necessary condition for the political accommodation of ethnic and cultural groups in a multinational state. Since most states are in fact multinational, the consociational model is an appropriate liberal solution to the problems of nationalism in these states. The theory of consociational democracy postulated by Lijphart states that certain structural conditions are favourable to its adoption and success. Others, such as Horowitz, give different and more flexible models and strategies for political accommodation.

No definite conclusions can be drawn about these models and strategies, however, and in the theory presented here 'political accommodation' is left unspecified, and no further 'sufficient conditions' are listed. It is likely that two aspects of such accommodation are needed. First, no one nation should have a majority position in the state government or legislature; and second, each nation should have a measure of autonomy within its territory. In this simplified formula, it is possible to find some form of accommodation or consociational system in many multinational states. These typically possess multinational coalition governments, or representation of nationals in central government, and proportionality of offices at the centre, with federalism or devolution for the different nations.

Success in consociationalism seems to depend on the cohesion of the national 'segments' whereby national leaders command the support of their nations. It is also likely that the party system and voting pattern will be based not on state-wide competitive parties, but on parties competing for support only within their own nation, or on national sections of state-wide parties.

The instability of most consociational systems, however, may point to the fragility of any democratic alternative to the orthodox nation-state. Authoritarian regimes are often used to hold down unsatisfied nationalisms in a multinational state. Yet consociational democracies do work, and they are an alternative to the break-up of multinational states into separate nation-states. The theory of nationalism presented here makes no judgment as to which form of state is more desirable, the nation-state or the consociational multinational state. But it can indicate which is more appropriate to the circumstances.

In international relations, the theory of the politics of national-ism and ethnicity postulates that national homogeneity is a necessary condition for strong internal support of a state's foreign policy (Chap-ter 10). A multinational state runs the risk of losing the support of its national minorities, unless the political system is imbued with consoc-iational features. The alternatives are assimilation or authoritarianism, and neither is easily attained.

Despite this, patriotism and xenophobia are easily mobilised by governments, since the state structure provides a ready-made ingroup-outgroup framework leading to the potential for psychological hos-tilities between the citizens of different states. Internationalism and supranationalism have proved to be weak competitors to 'official nationalism', and they usually take the limited form of economic 'com-mon markets' and military alliances. Attempts to move beyond these to genuine supranational federations have so far been unsuccessful. Progress towards supranationalism ('integration') encounters the same obstacles as progress towards 'official nationalism' in multinational states. Such states can mobilise nationalism successfully only when there is social homogeneity, or consociationalism, or a strong external threat. Supranational bodies are less likely than states to establish these conditions, although some progress towards 'regional' (international) integration has been made, e.g., in the European Community.

In times of war, hatreds between opposing states and nations become extreme, and appeals to nationalism are remarkably successful. The fact that so many people make the 'supreme sacrifice' of dying for their nation is testimony to a special force shaping human behaviour. Explaining that force must be the principal task of any theory of nationalism. The theory presented here gives a framework which can help to provide an answer to that and other questions in the politics of nationalism and ethnicity.

Synopsis of Theory

Each section represents a 'building-block' of the theory, and each 'building-block' is built upon the foundations of its predecessor. The columns are similarly linked, moving progressively from left to right to denote 'necessary' and 'sufficient' conditions. The relevant academic disciplines are given in brackets in the 'building-block' column.

'Building-block'	Necessary condition for	Sufficient condition for
1. Human nature and political behaviour:		
Instinctive behaviour (*sociobiology*)	Selfishness; altruism Social bonding; 'Kin selection'; inclusive fitness'. Nepotism; slavery; genocide.	Ethnicity Ethnocentrism Xenophobia
(*neurophysiology, socio-linguistics*)	Language	'Mother tongues' (but language divisions also require a political and social explanation)
Deliberate behaviour (*social psychology*)	Individual and group 'rational self-interest' Responses to displacement, frustration, etc	'Realistic group conflict (ingroup/outgroup) 'Irrational' ingroup/ outgroup hostility
2. Ideas and ideologies: (*Philosophy; sociology*)	The idea of the nation The idea of nationalism The idea of race	Nationalism as ideology Racism, Nazism, Fascism, anti-Semitism, White Supremacy, caste systems. (*)

* The presence and strength of these ideologies varies with the political circumstances.

171

'Building-block'	*Necessary condition for*	*Sufficient condition for*
3. Cultural, economic, social and political change:		
(history, anthropology, sociology, economics, political science)		
The sovereign state	The 'nation-state' The multinational state	'Official nationalism'
Democracy/popular sovereignty Economic, cultural and political homogeneity		
		'Social nationalism'
Economic, social, and political inequalities/ displacements in a multi-national state or colonial empire	Nationalist/ethnic/ racial conflicts 'Cultural Division of Labour' Uneven development Internal Colonialism	'Ethnic nationalism' Wars of national liberation Ethnic politics
'Post-industrial society'	New nationalities/ ethnicities 'Post-materialist values'	Nationalist and ethnic politics
Competitive politics	Formation of organis- ations and parties. Voting for nationalist parties. Nationalist/ ethnic leaders	
'Regime change'	Strong capability of nationalist and ethnic parties/movements	

'Building-block'	Necessary condition for	Sufficient condition for
4. Consociational democracy *(political science)*	Political accommod-ation of ethnic and cultural groups	
5. Nationalism in International Relations *(political science)* *Linkage between internal national and ethnic homogeneity and external politics:*		
(a) internal national/ ethnic tensions	Foreign policy weakly supported internally	Weak nationalism in state's international relations
(b) homogeneous nation-state, or consociational democracy	Foreign policy strongly supported internally	Strong nationalism in state's international relations
Patriotism and xenophobia	International state system. Relative weakness of international and supranational bodies	Loyalty and 'supreme sacrifice' of citizens in times of war

Bibliography

Adorno, T., *et al.* (1950) *The Authoritarian Personality* (New York: Harper & Row).

Alderman, G. (1983) *The Jewish Community in British Politics* (Oxford: Oxford University Press).

Alderman, G. (1989) *London Jewry and London Politics 1889–1986* (London: Routledge).

Alter, P. (1989) *Nationalism* (London: Edward Arnold).

Anderson, B. (1983) *Imagined Communities. Reflections on the Origin and Spread of Nationalism* (London: Verso/NLB).

Anwar, M. (1986) *Race and Politics: Ethnic Minorities and the British Political System* (London: Tavistock).

Arasaratnam, S. (1987) 'Sinhala–Tamil Relations in Modern Sri Lanka (Ceylon)', in Boucher *et al.* (eds) (1987).

Banac, I. (1984) *The National Question in Yugoslavia. Origins History Politics* (Ithaca and London: Cornell University Press).

Banton, M. (1983) *Racial and ethnic competition* (Cambridge University Press).

Barnard, F. (ed.) (1969) *J. G. Herder on social and political culture* (Cambridge University Press).

Barth, F. (ed.) (1969) *Ethnic Groups and Boundaries: the Social Organization of Cultural Difference* (London: George Allen & Unwin).

Berki, R. N. (1986) *State, Class, Nation* (Hull University Press).

Berry, C. J. (1981) 'Nations and Norms', *The Review of Politics*, vol. 43, pp. 75–87.

Birch, A. H. (1989) *Nationalism and National Integration* (London: Unwin Hyman).

Boucher, J., Landis, D., Clark, K. A. (eds) (1987) *Ethnic Conflict. International Perspectives* (Newbury Park, California: Sage).

Brand, J. A. (1985) 'Nationalism and the Noncolonial periphery: a discussion of Scotland and Catalonia', in Tiryakian and Rogowski (eds) (1985).

Brass, P. (ed.) (1985) *Ethnic Groups and the State* (London & Sydney: Croom Helm).

Breuilly, J. (1982) *Nationalism and the State* (Manchester University Press).

Connor, Walker (1984) *The National Question in Marxist–Leninist Theory and Strategy* (Princeton University Press).

Dawkins, R. (1989) *The Selfish Gene* (Oxford University Press), 2nd edn; 1st edn 1976.

Deutsch, K. W. (1966) *Nationalism and Social Communication: An Inquiry into the Foundations of Nationality* (Cambridge, Massachusetts: MIT Press), 2nd edn; 1st edn 1953.

Dogan, M. and Pelassy, D. (1984) *How to Compare Nations. Strategies in Comparative Politics* (Chatham, New Jersey: Chatham House).

Duncan, A. A. M. (1970) *The Nation of Scots and the Declaration of Arbroath (1320)* (London: Historical Association Pamphlet no. 75).

Eddy, J. and Schreuder, D. (eds) (1988) *The Rise of Colonial Nationalism. Australia, New Zealand, Canada and South Africa first assert their nationalities 1880–1914* (Sydney: Allen & Unwin).

Edwards, J. (1985) *Language, Society and Identity* (Oxford: Blackwell).

Enloe, C. E. (1973) *Ethnic Conflict and Political Development* (Boston: Little, Brown).

Esman, M. J. (ed.) (1977) *Ethnic Conflict in the Western World* (Ithaca and London: Cornell University Press).

Fishman, J. (1971–72) *Advances in the Sociology of Language* (The Hague: Mouton), vol. I, 1971; vol. II, 1972.

Fishman, J. (1973) *Language and Nationalism. Two Integrative Essays* (Rowley, Mass.: Newbury House).

Fishman J. (ed.) (1985) *The Rise and Fall of the Ethnic Revival: Perspectives on Language and Ethnicity* (Berlin, New York, Amsterdam: Mouton).

Fitzmaurice, J. (1985) *Québec and Canada. Past, Present and Future* (London: Hurst).

Forbes, H. D. (1985) *Nationalism, Ethnocentrism, and Personality* (Chicago and London: University of Chicago Press).

Glazer, N. and Moynihan, D. P. (eds) (1975) *Ethnicity. Theory and Experience* (Cambridge, Mass.: Harvard University Press).

Gellner, E. (1983) *Nations and Nationalism* (Oxford: Blackwell).

Gorbachev, M. (1988) *Perestroika* (London: Fontana/Collins).

Greenberg, S. B. (1980) *Race and State in Capitalist Development. Comparative Perspectives* (New Haven and London: Yale University Press).

Haas, E. B. (1958) *The Uniting of Europe. Political, Social and Economic Forces, 1950–1957* (Stanford University Press).

Halliday, F. and Alavi, H. (eds) (1988), *State and Ideology in the Middle East and Pakistan* (Basingstoke: Macmillan Education).

Hamilton, W. D. (1964) 'The genetical evolution of social behaviour', *Journal of Theoretical Biology*, vol. 7, pp. 1–52.

Harding, N. (ed.) (1984) *The State in Socialist Society* (London: Macmillan)

Hechter, M. (1975) *Internal Colonialism. The Celtic fringe in British national development 1536–1966* (London: Routledge & Kegan Paul).

Hechter, M. (1985) 'Internal Colonialism Revisited', in Tiryakian and

Rogowski (eds) (1985).

Herder, J. G. (1772) *On the Origin of Language* (see Barnard).

Hinsley, F. H. (1973) *Nationalism and the International System* (London: Hodder & Stoughton).

Hobsbawm, E. (1990) *Nations and Nationalism since 1780* (Cambridge University Press).

Horowitz, D. L. (1985) *Ethnic Groups in Conflict* (Berkeley, Los Angeles and London: University of California Press).

Hroch, M. (1985) *Social preconditions of national revival in Europe. A comparative analysis of the social composition of patriotic groups among the smaller European nations* (Cambridge University Press).

Hughes, Arnold (1981) 'The Nation-State in Black Africa', in Tivey (ed.) (1981)

Inglehart, R. F. (1977) *The Silent Revolution: Changing Values and Political Style among Western Publics* (Princeton University Press).

Isaacs, H. R. (1975) *Idols of the Tribe* (New York: Harper & Row).

Keating, M. (1988) *State and Regional Nationalism. Territorial Politics and the European State* (Hemel Hempstead: Harvester Wheatsheaf).

Kedourie, E. (1960) *Nationalism* (London: Hutchinson).

Kilson, M. (1975) 'Blacks and Neo-Ethnicity in American Political Life', in Glazer and Moynihan (1975).

Kirk-Greene, A. H. M. (1988) '"A Sense of Belonging": The Nigerian Constitution of 1979 and the Promotion of National Loyalty', *Journal of Commonwealth and Comparative Politics*, vol. XXVI, no. 2, pp. 158–72.

Kohn, H. (1944) *The Idea of Nationalism* (New York: Macmillan). 1945 corrected edition used.

Krejci, J. and Velimsky, V. (1981) *Ethnic and Political Nations in Europe* (London: Croom Helm).

Laponce, J. A. (1985) 'Protecting the French Language in Canada: From Neurophysiology to Geography in Politics: The Regional Imperative', *Journal of Commonwealth and Comparative Politics*, vol. XXIII, pp. 157–70.

LeVine, R. A. and Campbell, D. T. (1972) *Ethnocentrism: Theories of Conflict, Ethnic Attitudes and Group Behaviour* (New York: Wiley).

Lijphart, A. (1968) *The Politics of Accommodation. Pluralism and Democracy in the Netherlands* (Berkeley: University of California Press).

Lijphart, A. (1977) *Democracy in Plural Societies: A Comparative Exploration* (New Haven: Yale University Press).

Lijphart, A. (1984) *Democracies. Patterns of Majoritarian and Consensus Government in Twenty-One Countries* (New Haven and London: Yale University Press).

Lijphart, A. (1985) *Power-sharing in South Africa* (Berkeley: University of California Press).

Linz, J. (1985) 'From Primordialism to Nationalism' in Tiryakian and

Rogowski (eds) (1985).

McAuley, M. (1984) 'Nationalism and the Soviet Multi-ethnic State', in Harding (ed.) (1984).

McGarry, J. and Noel, S. J. R. (1989) 'The Prospects for Consociational Democracy in South Africa', *Journal of Commonwealth and Comparative Politics*, vol. XXVII, pp. 3–22.

McRae, K. (ed.) (1974) *Consociational Democracy. Political Accommodation in Segmented Societies* (Toronto: McClelland and Stewart).

Manor, J. (1990) 'How and Why Liberal and Representative Politics Emerged in India', *Political Studies*, vol. XXXVIII, pp. 20-38.

Mayall, J. (1990) *Nationalism and International Society* (Cambridge University Press).

Mazzini, G. (1835) *Faith and the Future*. Also later Preface to same (1850), in W. Clarke (ed.), *Essays: Selected from the Writings, Literary, Political and Religious, of Joseph Mazzini* (London: Walter Scott).

Miles, R. (1982) *Racism and Migrant Labour* (London: Routledge & Kegan Paul).

Mill, J. S. (1861) *Considerations on Representative Government*. In H. B. Acton's 1972 edn (London: J. M. Dent).

Minogue, K. (1967) *Nationalism* (London: Methuen).

Mitrany, D. (1975) *The Functional Theory of Politics* (London: Martin Robertson).

Moreno, L. (1988) 'Scotland and Catalonia: The Path to Home Rule' in D. McCrone and A. Brown (eds), *The Scottish Government Yearbook 1988* (Edinburgh: Unit for the Study of Government in Scotland).

Morris, D. (1981) *The Soccer Tribe* (London: Jonathan Cape).

Motyl, A. J. (1987) *Will the Non-Russians Rebel? State, Ethnicity, and Stability in the USSR* (Ithaca: Cornell University Press).

Mughan, A. (1979) 'Modernization and regional relative deprivation: towards a theory of ethnic conflict', in Sharpe (1979).

Page, E. (1978) 'Michael Hechter's internal colonial thesis: some theoretical and methodological problems', *European Journal of Political Research*, vol. 6, no. 3 (September 1978), pp. 295–317.

Pappalardo, A. (1981) 'The Conditions for Consociational Democracy: a Logical and Empirical Critique', *European Journal of Political Research*, vol. 9, pp. 365–90.

Rex, J. and Mason, D. (eds) (1986) *Theories of Race and Ethnic Relations* (Cambridge University Press).

Reynolds, V., Falger, V. S. E., and Vine, I. (eds) (1987) *The Sociobiology of Ethnocentrism. Evolutionary dimensions of xenophobia, discrimination, racism and nationalism* (London and Sydney: Croom Helm).

Riggs, Fred W. (ed.) (1985) *Ethnicity: INTERCOCTA Glossary. Concepts and terms used in Ethnicity Research* (pilot edition) (Honolulu: Dept. of Political Science, University of Hawaii).

Rokkan, S. and Urwin, D. W. (eds) (1982) *The Politics of Territorial*

Identity. Studies in European Regionalism (London: Sage).

Rokkan, S. and Urwin, D. W. (1983) *Economy, Territory, Identity: Politics of West European Peripheries* (London: Sage).

Rothschild, J. (1981) *Ethnopolitics. A Conceptual Framework* (New York: Columbia University Press).

Seton-Watson, H. (1977) *Nations and States. An Enquiry into the Origins of Nations and the Politics of Nationalism* (London: Methuen).

Sharpe, L. J. (ed.) (1979) *Decentralist trends in western democracies* (London and Beverly Hills: Sage).

Shaw, R. P. and Wong, Y. (1989) *Genetic Seeds of Warfare. Evolution, Nationalism and Patriotism* (Boston: Unwin Hyman).

Sherif, M. *et. al.* (1961) *Inter-group Conflict and Cooperation* (Oklahoma: Norman).

Smith, A. D. (1983) *Theories of Nationalism* (London: Duckworth) 2nd edn; 1st edn 1971.

Smith, A. D. (1986) *The Ethnic Origins of Nations* (Oxford: Blackwell).

Sullivan, J. (1988) *ETA and Basque Nationalism. The Fight for Euskadi, 1890–1986* (London and New York: Routledge).

Tinker, Hugh (1981) 'The Nation-State in Asia', in Tivey (ed.) (1981).

Tiryakian, E. A. and Rogowski, R. (eds) (1985) *New Nationalisms of the Developed West* (Boston, London, Sydney: Allen & Unwin).

Tivey, L. (ed.) (1981) *The Nation-State. The formation of modern politics* (Oxford: Martin Robertson).

van den Berghe, P. L. (1981) *The Ethnic Phenomenon* (New York, Amsterdam, Oxford: Elsevier).

Wolfe, Billy (1973) *Scotland Lives* (Edinburgh: Reprographia).

Young, C. (1976) *The Politics of Cultural Pluralism* (Madison: University of Wisconsin Press).

Index

179